CREATING

AUTHENTIC

VICTORIAN

ROOMS

For Emma

Designed by Gibson Parsons Design.
Text © 1995 by Elan and Susan Zingman-Leith. All rights reserved.
Illustrations and photographs © 1995 as attributed on pages 147–148.
© 1995 by Elliott & Clark Publishing. All rights reserved.
This book, or any portions thereof, may not be reproduced
in any form without written permission of the publisher.
Printed and bound in Hong Kong through Mandarin Offset.
Any inquiries should be directed to Elliott & Clark Publishing,
P.O. Box 21038, Washington, DC 20009-0538, telephone (202) 387-9805.

Library of Congress Cataloging-in-Publication Data

Zingman-Leith, Elan, 1951–
Creating authentic Victorian rooms / by Elan and Susan Zingman-Leith.
p. cm.
Includes index.
ISBN 1-880216-27-2
1. Victoriana in interior decoration. I. Zingman-Leith, Susan, 1950– II. Title.
NK2115.5.V53Z56 1995
747' .9—dc20 95-1024
CIP

CREATING AUTHENTIC VICTORIAN ROOMS

By

Elan and Susan Zingman-Leith

ELLIOTT & CLARK PUBLISHING
Washington, D.C.

TABLE OF CONTENTS

INTRODUCTION

This book was written to help the reader furnish and decorate Victorian period rooms. It is intended for both the homeowner and the professional. We shall explain how Victorians furnished their houses, why they made the decorating decisions that they did, and how to decorate your house authentically.

In any particular style, the furnishings that were designed to go in a house look good in their proper setting. It is also more challenging to find the right picture frame, the right lamp, and the right drapes than to use just any accessory that's handy. When you furnish your home, of course, you are free to do anything you want—it's your house. Even if you fill it with modern furniture, understanding the hows and whys of Victorian decorating can lead you to make choices that complement your old house rather than fight it.

For professionals furnishing a house museum, we hope this survey of Victorian decorating serves as a good starting point. Family photographs and documents, period magazines, decorating books, and catalogues help guide the restoration of a particular house, but we shall share the reasoning and feeling of the times that went into the Victorians' decorating decisions. A large portion of the illustrations for this book are from primary sources—Victorian catalogues and decorating manuals.

Unfortunately, it is absolutely impossible for a modern person to create a period room. Homeowners in the 1870s grew up seeing a very different world around them than we do. We cannot erase all of the patterns and objects seen in our lifetimes and force ourselves to see like a 19th-century person. What looks good to us is not what looked good to them. That's why a 1930s "colonial" room looks curiously 1930s-ish. It's why the movie *Gone With the Wind* does not really feel like the Civil War era.

Having said it's impossible, let's talk about why it's worth trying anyway. Even though the rooms will look curiously 1990s-ish to future generations, there is no better choice than to furnish a room in the era and style of its construction. Many Victorian rooms had their ceilings lowered and their details stripped during the 1950s and 1960s in a desperate attempt to make them modern. A Victorian room cannot be made into a modern one. The attempt will only make it look sad and vandalized. On the other hand, each era can be appreciated for what it has to offer—the classic simplicity of a Greek Revival parlor or the cozy busyness of a Queen Anne hall. Rooms can be furnished and decorated appropriately and made to look comfortable with themselves, not straining to be something they cannot be.

This book is organized by styles in chronological order. We believe that it is important to realize what the "taste of the time" was when trying to create a period room. It is also essential to adopt a point of view, to be a particular character with tastes and preferences. Victorian rooms were not created by averages and bland, safe choices. Nineteenth-century styles in interior decoration had great meaning to people at the time—whether to confirm their place in the new order of society or to look back nostalgically at old values. The increasing pace of change during the second half of the 19th century caused people to feel the need for new styles to express their evolving roles. These styles represented competing world-views, the remnants of which we still live with today. The Industrial Revolution not only created the need for new styles but also supplied the means by providing machine-made furniture and finishes.

We've chosen to create a period house in our bed and breakfast and have found it very satisfying. In 1989 we bought an 1880s house in Cape May, New Jersey. Our house had most of its architectural features intact but none of the finishes and furnishings, so we had to decide how to decorate it. We chose to make a period interior, including very little that predates the construction of the house and nothing except necessities (plumbing and electricity) from the 20th century. This was one of three choices we might have made.

The first choice is the way most often taken by bed-and-breakfast owners and decorators—the aesthetic approach. This means treating the furniture as artistic objects, deciding whether you find them attractive, and combining them in ways you think beautiful regardless of their historic style. This approach sometimes mixes antiques from different eras as well as modern furnishings. Furnishing a Victorian house this way can result in a beautiful interior, or not, depending on the decorator, but it always results in a house that looks like the time in which it was furnished, not when it was built. Another disadvantage of this approach is that the furniture used this way has only one layer of meaning—its design to modern eyes. The other implications historic furniture can have would be lost: what the furniture says about the taste and social position of the people who originally chose it, how they lived from day to day, how they wanted to be regarded by their contemporaries, and how these messages are carried out in wallpaper, lamps, rugs, chairs, and pictures.

The second choice is the "organic" approach. Real historic houses that have been lived in continuously and never stripped don't look as if they were furnished all at once. We have seen several historic houses like this, with 1840s Gothic Revival walls, 1860s Rococo Revival chairs, 1890s Colonial Revival tables, 1920s sofas, and 1940s family portraits. When the house is significant because it was the home of a particular family (the Lincoln house in Vermont or Franklin D. Roosevelt's Hyde Park in New York), all of these furnishings are noteworthy because of their associations. Without the connection to the important owner, however, this approach has less to recommend it. The house may or may not be attractive or interesting. Moreover, houses like this are survivals; they cannot be convincingly created.

The third approach is to create a period interior. This means picking a time (either when the house was built or a later significant time) and developing a point of view. Start by finding out all you can about the style and date of your house. Examine the woodwork—baseboards, door and window casings, mantel and overmantel, and so on—for clues as to the original intention of the builders. Look for bits of old wallpaper stuck behind moldings and, perhaps, even send away paint samples for color analysis. If the old wallpaper has been stripped, look for the ghost of the pattern or color in the plaster. Look for scars of missing picture moldings, portière rods, and hardware. Go through the house and note every little alteration. When you put them on a plan, small things like cuts in the baseboard will turn up on both sides of a wall, giving you evidence that a door used to be there. Examine the walls in raking light, and old door and window openings will become clear; missing ceiling medallions and cornices will pop out.

Our house is a seaside summer cottage, so our point of view in restoring the house was that of a middle-class, urban family in the 1880s. The woodwork is reeded Aesthetic style, and the original overmantel mirror is Eastlake style as well. Because the 1870s and 1880s were a period of great design reform, we have chosen a point of view that would have been "artistic" or "aesthetic" for its time, rather than comfortably conventional. By the time of the construction of our house, the radical decorating movements of the 1870s might have worked their way down to the sort of people who inhabited our house and affected their choice of wallpaper, rugs, furniture, and even hardware, china, and silver.

While traveling around the United States visiting house museums, we compare them to our local house museum, the Physick Estate, and to our own house. Some historic houses are wonderfully convincing and seem lived-in and vibrant. Others seem to be sterile set-pieces displaying furniture but not redolent of the lives of their inhabitants. We believe the difference to be the presence or absence of a "point of view." Everywhere you look, you should be able to see that the person who chose a particular vase would also be likely to pick that pillow and that picture.

Do not be misled by the style organization of this book into thinking that most 19th-century homeowners cared deeply about consistency. Especially when contemporary styles had similar messages,

Victorians mixed elements with abandon. Not only did Victorians combine contemporary styles, but they constantly updated their houses, adding new purchases to existing older furnishings. As long as you keep in mind to what era and taste you are decorating your room (this is a bohemian, artistic house in the 1880s, or this is a substantial, middle-class house in the 1860s), you can successfully mix both styles and periods in creating an authentic historic interior.

There are, however, two things to guard against: anachronisms and randomness. It is very unlikely that an important public room in a middle-class, urban house was ever furnished with a whole suite of furniture in a style that was 30 years out-of-date when the house was built. An 1880s Queen Anne house furnished with an 1830s American Empire parlor suite would have been bizarre. An 1890s Colonial Revival house furnished with 1860s Rococo Revival settees was highly unusual. Although people often kept furniture for a long time and updated interiors with accessories and fabrics, they did not display family antiques or heirlooms until the Colonial Revival era. An 1860s parlor would not have had Grandma's Chippendale secretary bookcase proudly on view. There were no spinning wheels and dry sinks until the 1890s Colonial Revival enshrined these objects as icons of good taste. Grandma's old furniture would have been put to good use in the lesser bedrooms and servants' quarters.

Randomness is the harder pitfall to avoid. You see an Art Deco lamp at an antique shop or a 1920s desk that is so cheap. Before long, the interior you are furnishing is a personal collection of favorite objects. This approach is fine in your home, but you should not also pretend that you are creating a period interior. In an historic interior that was lived in for a long time, there were usually several redecorations. In those rooms, however, there is usually a preponderant style dating from one of the redecorations. There may be some leftovers from the earlier incarnations of the room, and there may be some later purchases, but there is almost always the feeling of a particular period, or perhaps two periods—not five, six, or seven.

In general, if there is evidence that the historic owners lived with furnishings from several periods, say an 1870s Aesthetic Movement interior with 1880s Renaissance Revival mantels and 1900s French wallpaper, it is best to put yourself in the point of view of the person doing the last redecoration. If you put in new French-style wallpaper in 1900 and did not rip out the baseboards and mantelpiece from the 1870s and 1880s, were you likely to buy new rugs, tablecloths, and picture frames? People often modernize with wallpaper, drapes, and furniture, but hardly ever rip out door and window casings. This kind of mixing should not serve as an excuse for combining tastes that were unlikely to coexist. The peacock feathers and pampas grass of the 1880s were hopelessly old-fashioned by 1910. The black-and-scarlet color schemes of the 1830s parlor would never have passed muster in an 1860s parlor. An 1860s baby blue bergère would not have been welcome in an 1880s Aesthetic library.

CREATING

AUTHENTIC

VICTORIAN

ROOMS

GREEK REVIVAL / AMERICAN EMPIRE: 1835–1850s

The general impression of an American Empire interior to modern eyes is very different from what came before and what followed. Preceding it, the Federal style was extremely elegant. As an American version of the neoclassical style made famous by the work of the Adam brothers in England, the style relied upon elongated, attenuated ornament based on Roman models. In plaster work, the Federal style favored finely molded ellipses formed of swags, beading, or shallow fluting. The furniture, popularly known as Hepplewhite, Sheraton, and Duncan Phyffe, tends to be slim and elegant with tapered legs and finely drawn marquetry designs ornamenting its surfaces. Two changes occurred during the late years of the Federal style, as shown in Duncan Phyffe's furniture: the number of dolphins, eagle talons, and lion paws carved as furniture feet increased, and the exaggerated refinement of the late 18th century became slightly less popular.

Greek Revival is the name given to the architectural style of the 1830s through the 1850s that looked to ancient Greece for its inspiration. American Empire is the name for the furniture that was produced at the same time with the same inspiration. Americans considered the Greek Revival style to be particularly suited to American civilization. They reasoned that the Greeks invented democracy and America was becoming more democratic. By electing Andrew Jackson president in 1828 instead of John Quincy Adams, Americans rejected the old representatives of the patrician, elite Founding Fathers and chose the Western, common man. The strong feeling in the country that the frontier was changing the American character expressed itself in the Greek Revival style. Like the architecture, Greek

Revival/American Empire furniture was middle-class, honest, and plain.

Edgar De Noailles Mayhew in *A Documentary History of American Interiors* comments on the popularity of all things Greek:

> *Further evidence of America's vision of the appropriateness of Greek and Roman models is to be found in the names of cities settled during the period. As the Erie Canal made access to New York State and the West easier, new towns appeared, and the abundance of classical names is overwhelming: Troy, Utica, Rome, Ithaca, Syracuse, Carthage, Corinth and Hannibal.*

Some of the characteristics of the American Empire or Greek Revival style are very Victorian: it was essentially a middle-class rather than upper-class style; it included the introduction of machine-made rather than handmade furniture; and it coincided with the waning of regional styles in furniture making in America. Some of the characteristics of the American Empire style are very un-Victorian: the interiors are noticeably spare, uncluttered, and severe; and the furniture is still lined up against the walls in the 18th-century manner, unlike all the styles that follow it.

Imagine an American Empire interior of the 1840s. The public floor of a row house usually consisted of two parlors and a dining room with the kitchen in an "L" in back or in the basement under the dining room. The walls of the parlor were probably plain paint, either white, putty, or scarlet. The furnishings consisted of a matched set of mahogany-veneered seating furniture arranged against opposite walls of the room in mirror image rows. If a *récamier* (a one-armed sofa

American Empire récamier.

Round Greek Revival center table.

Klismos chair.

named for Madame Récamier in Jacques Louis David's painting) sat against one wall, there was likely to be a twin on the opposite wall. The middle of the room was dominated by a large, probably round, center table with a lamp, a Bible, and a suitable book ornamenting its mahogany-veneered surface. The piers between the windows were taken up by pier tables or game tables, which could be pulled out for card parties. The mirrors above the pier tables were likely to be ogee mirrors about one and a half feet by three feet with broad, simple, mahogany-veneered frames. The major furniture was supplemented by a few light chairs and a sewing table. The light chairs were often klismos type with sabre-shaped legs and a low, horizontal back rail, or some classical variation with a lobed back rail and vase-shaped splat, all in mahogany. The furniture in the room was upholstered to match, and the overwhelmingly favorite cloth was black horsehair. The window curtains all matched and were almost certain to be scarlet or maroon rep drapes with white glass-curtains underneath. If there was one, the pelmet above the drapes was relatively plain, consisting of a simple box or swag and jabot.

FURNITURE

What is really noteworthy about American Empire furniture is its monumentality. This furniture did not rely upon carving, reeding, or fluting for its beauty. Instead it consisted of impressive silhouettes sheathed in crotch-grain, mahogany veneers. A secretary bookcase might feature a pedimented top or a large, ogee cornice. A chest of drawers or sideboard often displayed large, vertical volutes flanking the drawers or perhaps a pair of Ionic columns. A bed might be a sleigh bed with enormous S-curved head and footboards covered in veneer.

American Empire furniture was affordable because the underlying material was pine, and new power saws could cut lots of mahogany veneer from a tree that previously would have provided only a few boards.

WALLS AND CEILINGS

Wallpaper does play a part in the American Empire style, although it was not nearly as important as it became later in the century. Before this period, only the wealthiest Americans used wallpaper. The parlor, dining room, hall, or best bedroom of an 18th-century or early 19th-century house might be papered. The paper was probably imported, hand-painted, Chinese wallpaper or one of the French, printed, panoramic views called scenics. The scenic French wallpapers of the early 19th century continued to be popular through the middle of the century. During the 1840s, however, a shift occurred in the way they were used. Before the 1840s, the panorama, or *paysage panoramique,* was usually continuous around the room. After the 1840s, the room was generally divided into compartments by using wallpaper made to look like pilasters, cornices, and balustrades. The scenes then fit into the panels left between the pilasters as though the landscape were being viewed through a classical loggia.

The arms of this sofa are thoroughly Greek, while the legs are American eagles.

In *Wallpapers in Historic Preservation,* author Catherine Frangiamore emphasizes the long-lasting influence of French design:

> French style dominated the American wallpaper trade during the first 70 years of the 19th century. In the early part of the century bright, strongly colored, even gaudy, Empire styles … vied for attention with spectacular non-repeating "views" and "landscape" papers.

Several other types of wallpaper joined the scenic panorama in American popular taste during the 1840s. One consisted of wide, vertical, alternating stripes of color and white, or off-white. The white stripe was ornamented with columns of bouquets and sprigs of flowers or small landscapes. These alternating stripe-and-flower papers were frequently crowned at the top of the room by a narrow border of flower and swag patterned paper, often flocked. These papers were usually French. Stripe-and-flower paper may have had some low periods, but it has been in continuous production in America from the 1840s to the present, with especially popular decades in the early 20th-century Colonial Revival and again in the French Revival of the 1940s.

The left-hand wall shows an ashlar block patterned wallpaper often used for hallways from the 1840s onward. The right side features an 1880s Aesthetic Movement dado.

Another wallpaper pattern first made popular during this period is the gathered fabric type. Many of these papers look like continuous, Austrian window shades with vertical panels gently gathered by tapes into swagged folds. This illusion of a room completely hung with shirred fabric walls was first used by Napoléon Bonaparte at Malmaison to create a *faux* campaign tent in the palace. That is the reason for its classical associations and subsequent appropriateness to a Greek Revival interior. Other fabric-pattern papers include some where a panel of fabric appears to be stretched between rods at the top and bottom of the room and gathered into a knot or medallion at the center. These papers were harder to use because the height and width of the panels had to match the dimensions of the room or the pattern wouldn't work. Consequently, they were never as popular as the continuous-pattern papers.

Wallpaper imitating stone blocks was used almost exclusively for entry halls. The size of the blocks varied from tiny (about two inches long) to a realistic size. The blocks imitated stone, such as marble and limestone, or were decorated with anthemions, rosettes, or Greek keys. The fashion for these papers began in the American Empire period but persisted through much of the 19th century. Yet another kind of illusionistic wallpaper introduced in the 1840s could be found in any room in the house: woodgrain papers, which were printed to look like oak, maple, or mahogany, and have continued in use to the present day.

Finally, there was another class of wallpapers called *irisé* (after Iris, goddess of the rainbow) or rainbow papers. Produced by Zuber in France during the 1840s, these papers featured bands of color shading from light to dark, much like the ingrain carpets and jacquard coverlets that were also popular at the time. It must have been stunning (literally) when the rainbow carpets, wallpaper, and coverlets were used together.

According to Catherine Frangiamore:

A late 18th century style that lasted far into the 19th century featured the use of a plain solid shade of coloring applied to wallpaper, usually in green or in blue but available in other colors as well. These papers were called "plain papers" and were usually advertised with "rich" or "elaborate" borders …. Walls painted a solid color were also embellished with wallpaper borders; the "plain papers" had one advantage over paint—they hid the cracks.

How common was wallpaper in American Empire houses? Certainly much more common than it had been in the 18th century when it was printed with wood blocks onto sheets that were then glued together into strips. During the 19th century, the French invented continuous rollers made of steel with engraved patterns filled with wool to hold the inks. Continual improvements in wallpaper printing technology made papers much cheaper. Eventually, Americans and the English copied the French technology and patterns and produced even less expensive domestic papers. On the other hand, we should not confuse the 1840s with the 1880s. During the 1840s, the steam engine had just been developed. The Erie Canal had just been dug. The railroads were just beginning. The mid-century Industrial Revolution was only beginning, and there were not yet lots of factories churning out miles of paper. Also, there was not yet an audience of middle-class wage earners to buy the paper.

So, paint remained the most common wall finish in American Empire interiors. There was a strong tendency to all-gray color schemes in the Greek Revival. One explanation is that the style was disseminated through pattern books to people who never saw fancy, urban houses. The engravings in the pattern books were black and white, of course, so the general impression of gray walls was spread. There were plenty of scarlet walls, though, since white, gray, putty, and scarlet were the most popular colors for the parlor. At that time, however, a regular middle-class homeowner might have wallpapered the dining room or parlor in a French scenic. The hall might have been papered to resemble marble blocks. A best bedroom might have featured a French-style, stripe-and-flower pattern made in America. It was not likely, however, that one middle-class house would have had all of these. The era of every room in the house being papered did not arrive until the 1880s.

TRIM

The architectural moldings in a Greek Revival house were monumental. The baseboards, door and window casings, mantels, newel posts, and balustrades were all very substantial compared to the Federal style that preceded it. What does being substantial mean? First, the moldings were large. A door casing might be six or eight inches wide and a couple of inches deep. But more important is the character of the moldings. In the Federal style, these casings were often interrupted by many breaks in plane, by reeding, and by sharp arrises. In the Greek Revival, a broad flat casing might have a large, egg-shaped, ovolo molding near its outside edge and a shallow ogee near the inside edge. Even if they were the same size, the uninterrupted quality of the Greek Revival casing and the easy curve of the ogee molding, rather than the abrupt change in plane and direction of the earlier work, makes the Greek Revival version seem more monumental.

Anthemion.

The mantel was most likely to consist of a pair of wide flat pilasters supporting an even wider horizontal band. A small molding at the top of the pilasters represented the capital of a simple Doric or Tuscan order. A plain shelf completed the mantel, and there was no overmantel at all. This extremely basic post and lintel mantel was likely to have been marbleized wood in a modest house or marble in a wealthier residence. In a fancy example of a Greek Revival mantel, however, all this solidity might be relieved by an extremely delicate anthemion applied to the horizontal entablature. Sometimes the pilasters would be paneled or feature a double-

This American Empire mantel is monumental in scale with delicate anthemion appliqués. The wallpaper border imitates swagged fabric. The strong horizontal rails of the chair-backs are Greek.

Greek Revival door with battered surround.

This high-style parlor features double pairs of Ionic columns and huge-patterned carpet. The family portrait and horse-hair upholstery settee are perfect for this thoroughly Greek house.

anthemion appliqué. The effect of this extremely delicate, classical ornament applied to such chunky features was to emphasize just how substantial the mantel really was.

The room cornice of a Greek Revival parlor was substantial as well. The modillion brackets and deeply molded, acanthus leaf decoration that were so popular in the 18th century and would be so popular in the Italianate style were largely absent. A broad, simple, cove molding with an ovolo on the ceiling and another on the wall was all the cornice consisted of in most houses of this style. In a particularly elegant house, delicate water leaf moldings, fasces, and egg and darts might enliven the shadows at the top of the room.

The two parlors—the front or family parlor and the back or formal parlor—were not as different from each other as they came to be later in the century. The parlor was usually a straightforward, rectangular room with a pair of windows, a fireplace, a square opening to the hall, and another similar opening to the back parlor. In a high style house, the openings to the hall and the back parlor might be flanked by classical columns and topped by a full entablature. In a house of less wealthy owners, the columns might be replaced by pilasters. In a regular middle-class house, the door-surround could easily consist of an architrave with battered sides, ears, and a straight top. The fireplace in a Greek Revival parlor follows a similar pattern as the door-surrounds, varying from freestanding columns to attached pilasters. What all the trim in the room had in common was monumentality. The Doric columns or pilasters were fat. The entablature was heavy. The moldings were broad and spreading, based on wide ellipses.

FLOORS

Edgar De Noailles Mayhew notes in *A Documentary History of American Interiors* that by the time of the American Empire style, "floor coverings had become usual, even in the country. In well-to-do and middle-class houses, wall-to-wall carpets predominated ... [in] Scotch or ingrain carpet or the somewhat more expensive Wilton (cut pile) and Brussels (uncut pile) carpets .... The painted floor cloth remained as a means of protecting valuable dining room carpets ... as late as 1847."

The major pattern in the room was found on the floor. Ingrain carpet was the popular choice of the era. It was woven on narrow looms about 34 inches wide and sewn together in strips, then nailed around the perimeter of the floor. These wall-to-wall carpets featured patterns of wreaths, rosettes, and anthemions alternating in squares. The patterns were hard-edged and divided the floor into boxes. The colors repeated the scarlet, black, and gray theme of the room, often with sharp green or blue added for contrast. The designs of these carpets were enormous in scale, with individual rosettes or wreaths as much as three or four feet in diameter. Especially in a room with little pattern elsewhere, these carpets were astounding.

Ingrain carpets were introduced in the Greek Revival era and remained in use for the rest of the 19th century. As other types of carpet were made available, ingrains were relegated to upstairs and servants' rooms.

LIGHTING

The first point to remember about lighting in the Greek Revival room is that there was not much of it. As in the 18th century, there were candles. There are many Greek Revival candlestick designs in molded glass, some featuring dolphins or classical maidens. But, we should remember how expensive candles were and how unlikely it was for most people to have numerous candlesticks and burn lots of candles. These were not accessories for romantic dinners or well-furnished mantels but accompaniments to eye-straining letter-writing or figuring out household accounts.

Pressed glass candlestick with a classical dolphin.

The other mainstay of Greek Revival lighting was the whale-oil lamp. Whale oil began to be widely produced about 1800 and was of two types. The first was rendered from the blubber of the Greenland right whale. The second was sperm oil taken from a cavity in the head of the sperm whale. However, sperm oil was exorbitantly expensive and seldom used in private homes. The whale-oil lamp can be distinguished from the many other fluid-burning lamps by its font and burner. The glass font was small, usually about the size and shape of an upside-down pear. It was supported by a little metal post often in the shape of a column or a turned baluster. The column sat in a small, square, marble base. The glass font was fitted with a brass cap which held a brass burner. The sleeve for the wick was small, projecting only one-quarter inch above the cup, and held a round rope-shaped wick. A thumbscrew turned the wick up or down. This common type of oil lamp was sometimes called an agitable and was available from about 1800.

Molded glass oil lamp with pear-shaped font.

Argand burner with cylindrical wick.

The Argand burner was invented in 1780 by a Swiss chemist named Aimée Argand. It featured two nested hollow tubes with a tubular wick between them allowing air to come up the center. It was first used with sperm whale oil, and later the principle was applied to kerosene and gas lamps. The earliest American-made Argand burners date from 1825.

An alternative to the common oil lamp (agitable) and the more expensive Argand burner was the astral oil lamp. The astral lamp was also called sineumbra from the Latin *sine umbra* (without shadow). It was patented in 1843 and used an Argand-type, cylindrical burner. In an astral lamp, the burner was surrounded by a doughnut-shaped font so the font did not cast much of a shadow on the table. Astral or sineumbra lamps were also called solar lamps.

Even as late as 1860, people commonly burned lard in addition to whale oil and burning fluid. Lard smoked and smelled bad, but it was plentiful and cheap. Lamps specifically made for lard burning often have wide, flat wicks with the wick tube extending far down into the reservoir to help melt the lard. These lamps were usually simple and utilitarian. Solar lamps could also burn lard because of the proximity of the burner to the font.

In the 1840s a short-lived fashion developed for an insane invention called the burning fluid lamp. Whale oil was so expensive and other fats like tallow and lard so stinky and sooty that Isaiah Jennings came up with an alternative in 1830. Burning fluid was a mixture of alcohol and turpentine and burned cleanly with a strong light. Unfortunately, as the font emptied, the remaining fluid was so volatile that it filled the airspace with highly combustible fumes. Eventually the metal tube that held the wick would get hot enough to ignite the vapors, and the lamp would explode like a firebomb, showering the room with burning alcohol and turpentine. This may explain why they are so rare today in antique shops, and why their owners seldom made it to old age. Burning fluid was renamed camphene in 1839, but its flaws were unchanged. A burner specifically made for burning fluid can be recognized because it has no metal tube extending down into the font.

Sineumbra lamp with and without its shade, showing the doughnut shaped font.

Solar lamp with a metal font.

It often has two slim, conical wick tubes slanted away from each other to dissipate the heat and little caps for the tubes to keep the fluid from evaporating.

The first gasoliers date from the 1830s in the Greek Revival style, though gas did not become generally available until the 1850s and 1860s. A gasolier composed of concentric rings of glass prisms, called icicles, around a central pipe formed one of the earliest types of fixture and was going out of fashion by the late 1840s.

WINDOWS

The most common Greek Revival window was double-hung with six lights of glass in the upper sash and six in the lower. They were almost always painted white (a creamy white because of the yellow linseed oil in the paint). For most of the Greek Revival period, many people continued to use Venetian blinds as they had in the Federal period. Venetian blinds, incidentally, really did come from Venice and were made of wood with two or three vertical tapes. Otherwise, they were much the same as they are today.

The top of the window seldom sported a visible cornice. Instead, there was a relatively simple, pleated triangle of fabric at each jamb and a pleated swag across the top. This arrangement, called a swag and jabot, remained from the Federal period. A plain set of scarlet or maroon drapes might also be hung at the window. Consider the simplicity of this window treatment. The applied braids, rickrack, fringes, tassels, and other *passementerie* of the later 19th century had not yet

Venetian blinds and patterned window shades.

appeared. The drapes did not puddle on the floor, that is, trail on the floor in a decorative arrangement. The pelmets were not composed of layers of elaborately trimmed and gathered fabric. If there was a curtain underneath the drapes, it was probably sheer muslin. Paintings from this period make it clear that many middle-class parlors and dining rooms still did not have curtains at all.

One kind of practical curtain often seen in paintings of Greek Revival interiors is a kind of café curtain suspended from a small rod or string at the meeting rail and made of very light fabric such as cheesecloth, gauze, or muslin. This was the bug bar. Metal window screens were not invented until the 1880s, and, until then, people hung some version of mosquito or fly netting at the windows and around their beds.

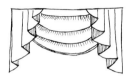

Swag and jabot.

PICTURES

We expect lots of pictures of classical antiquity in the Greek Revival interior, right? Wrong. Those Victorian pictures of Greece and Rome are all late 19th century. Greek Revival walls displayed few pictures, and those were most often portraits. Cut silhouettes remained popular from the 18th century. The pictures, hung with concealed cords (unlike later in the century), were displayed very high on the wall compared to today's taste. The most popular subjects were Grandpa and Grandma, followed by George and Martha Washington. In fact, George and Martha remained popular throughout the 19th century, supplemented later by Abraham Lincoln.

Edgar Mayhew describes the arrangement of pictures in a Greek Revival house:

A considerable number of small pictures or prints could be placed in balanced groupings, or a fair number of larger pictures could be placed singly around the wall. Toward the end of the period, single paintings with elaborate frames dominated whole walls.

BEDROOM

The general arrangement of an American Empire bedroom was different from that of the 18th-century bedroom. With the advent of heating stoves, fireplaces were no longer the only source of heat, so working bed curtains began to disappear. The tester bed that had been such a mainstay for hundreds of years came to be replaced by several new shapes.

One new kind of bedstead featured four substantial, mahogany-veneered posts at the corners with the headboard hung from two of the posts. The headboard was usually sheathed in bookmatched mahogany veneer and might feature a slightly pedimented top. This bed had endless variations in which the posts formed octagonal or Doric columns or were lathe-turned with ball finials.

Sleigh bed.

A second popular bed type was the sleigh bed. With tall, opposing, S-curved headboard and footboard, this kind of bed strongly resembled a French *lit en bateau* (boat bed). The head and footboards of a sleigh bed also resembled the arms of a late Federal settee blown up to massive scale.

A third type of Empire bed was much like a sleigh bed, except that the tall, equal-sized head and footboards were straight. This was called a *lit à la Polonaise* in French and, in the United States, was just an inexpensive variation of the sleigh bed.

Now that bed curtains were no longer needed for warmth, they became decorative. Sometimes a ring or crown suspended above the bed supported a pair of curtains draped from head to foot over a sleigh bed or a *lit à la Polonaise* arranged sideways in the room. A bed with its headboard against the wall might have curtains draped over the head of the bed with the curtain support either part of the bed or independent of it.

Lit à la Polonaise with separately supported decorative hangings.

Greek Revival chests of drawers varied from simple to ornate, but they were all very substantial. At their simplest, they were plain cases with mahogany-veneered drawer fronts and wide, button-shaped, wooden knobs. Additional decorations might be glove boxes taking up the back half of the top, or long veneered volutes forming the stiles of the carcass, or faceted glass knobs instead of plain wood. At their fanciest, the stiles of the carcass were faced with fully rounded, carved colonettes, the knobs were large hobnail glass in clear or white color, and the mirror was supported by an elaborate, mahogany-veneered wishbone attached to the dresser top.

A simple Empire dresser with glove boxes and a wishbone-shaped mirror support.

Also, the Empire bedroom usually contained a chair or two, a table or two for working and reading, and, perhaps, a récamier. There were, of course, chamber pots, combs and brushes, and other *articles de toilette*. The walls of a Greek Revival bedroom were most likely painted, usually a light color. Curtains, if there were any, were lightweight, washable cottons such as calico or muslin. Pictures were few and most likely portraits. The floor may have been covered with straw matting, sometimes summer and winter, with small bedside rugs—druggets, rag rugs, or pieces of ingrain.

FRENCH STYLE / ROCOCO REVIVAL: 1850s–1860s

During the 1850s and 1860s, the world changed enough to make the Greek Revival parlor seem old-fashioned and out-of-date. What had seemed so forthright and democratic 20 or 30 years before now looked too plain and stiff to be really elegant. Technological advances in the iron and coal industries, improvements in the steam engine, and the proliferation of the railroad supported an urban in-dustrialization boom in the 1850s and 1860s. Many people who would have been farmers in the 1830s and 1840s found that they could work as factory managers or clerks in offices. The separation between the daily life of men and women, which reached its height later in the century, was well under way.

There are two major differences between the Rococo Revival room of the 1850s and 1860s and what went before. The first is obvi-ous—French design became fashionable in furniture, wallpaper, and fabric. The second is revolutionary—informality was introduced for the first time in half a century.

Let's deal with informality first. During the middle of the 18th century, rooms were not thought of as single-purpose. Tables were moved around the house as needed. The central hall might serve as a dining room for a large crowd. Supper might as easily be eaten in the bedroom or the drawing room or the kitchen. As the 18th century wore on, Federal era rooms came to be used more for only one ac-tivity. By the Greek Revival era, the furniture was perfectly arranged against the walls, and every activity had its appointed place. It was extremely formal and rigid.

Suddenly the whole house underwent a transformation. Women who formerly worked on the farm now spent their days in their own and other women's parlors, talking, doing needlework and handicrafts. Gathering to chat and to do light, "ladylike" work required moving the chairs away from the walls and grouping them conversationally around a carpet near the fireplace or parlor stove. The tight correspondence between the architecture and the furniture disappeared. Instead of two rock-hard, symmetrical settees facing each other across the room with a pier glass between the windows, now a curvy, comfortable loveseat and a couple of *fauteuils* might gather companionably in the middle of the room.

The Rococo Revival of the mid-19th century was based on the French, domestic Rococo of the mid-18th century. The French Rococo was created for aristocratic ladies in their *petits appartements*. It was a light, informal alternative to the heavy, bombastic style of the state rooms (the *grands appartements*). Those women, however, were not striving for status. Their style had a relaxed grace and restraint that was very different from the later Victorian revival. In the 1850s and 1860s, the decoration of houses came to be thought of as a feminine pursuit. Previously, a man was very involved in the furnishing of his house. Now, the matter was between a woman and her upholsterer, as Victorian decorators were called. The increasing gender separation of daily life led Victorian women to look for feminine sources for their motifs, so they looked to 18th-century France.

To understand what mid-19th-century folks found attractive, we have to put several modern concepts out of our minds: first, the idea that restraint is more tasteful than all-out ornament. The Victorians of the 1860s did not feel that too much ornamentation was tacky,

Rococo Revival fainting couch.

Rococo Revival settee with cabriole legs and an exaggeratedly curved back.

that decorations should be viewed against a plain surface, or that the space between objects and motifs was just as important as the things themselves. It's interesting to note that the favorite adjective of furniture salesmen at the time was "elegant," which we might take to mean restrained or edited to its essentials. Not so. When they said "elegant," they meant decorated or embellished. It is no wonder, then, that newly middle-class women striving for elegance applied Rococo motifs to every object and surface.

Second, we moderns have to ignore all of the freedom to create "artful" juxtapositions that came into fashion just after this period and is still the stock-in-trade of decorators today. Mid-century Victorians who used the Rococo style were rigidly conventional. Their aim was not to create an interior that was "artistic" or "original." They wanted interiors to be pretty (they would have said "elegant") in an absolutely predictable way. They wanted to be stylish in exactly the same way as other middle-class people were in order to confirm their membership in the club of middle-classness.

What really distinguishes the Rococo Revival parlor from both earlier and later periods is the arrangement of objects in the room. Before this period the tables, mantel, or piano were not laden with decorative objets d'art. After this period, the decorative objects were arranged in artful still lifes. During the Rococo style, objects were placed in symmetrical arrangements in matched sets.

The Rococo Revival was by far the most popular style of the Victorian era. Just as the Italianate house expressed the values of a self-confident, new middle class, the Rococo interior did the same. To modern eyes, there is a sort of nervousness in the Rococo Revival room. The counterbalanced S-curves of the chair legs and backs are repeated in the counterbalanced C-curves of the Aubusson-style carpet. They are repeated in the cartouches of the wallpaper and again in the pattern of the damask upholstery and draperies. All these curves and pattern without a plain surface or a straight line to rest on creates unease in the modern viewer, who is used to a moderate combination of plain surfaces and pattern and of plane surfaces and curves.

FURNITURE

The most famous Rococo Revival chairmaker was John Henry Belter, a German immigrant to New Jersey, who invented a new method of construction and, with it, a new aesthetic. Belter created a glorified plywood by gluing rosewood veneers into a curved-in-plan mold. Belter's plywood had the curve built into its structure and so was impossible to flatten out. A chair back so constructed was incredibly strong and could be pierced and carved into a pear-shaped wreath of roses and still support the weight of the heaviest Victorian burgher or matron. Belter's advance allowed chair backs to be undercut and carved more than had ever been possible. This change led to a volume of ornament that would be considered grotesque by modern standards, but magnificent by the standards of the time. Though Belter was extremely successful and made a lot of chairs, his furniture was expensive in its time and was really appropriate only for a well-off middle-class house or better. Most people furnishing their houses in this style had to content themselves with less ambitious versions.

We should make a note of a change in materials about this time. Through the 18th century, mahogany was the preferred wood for all fine furniture. Its dark red color and suitability for carving were highly prized. During the American Empire era, mahogany veneers used on case furniture brought the expensive wood within the reach of middle-class homeowners. By the mid-19th century, solid mahogany was becoming extremely expensive because the forests of Santo Domingo and Honduras were becoming depleted. Rosewood was found to be an acceptable substitute and continued the same appearance of rich, dark red wood tones with lots of carving.

The major characteristic of Rococo Revival furniture is, of course, the curves. Settees and chairs now stood on S-curved, cabriole legs. Both seats and backs became bulbous with S-curved, wooden outlines and tufted upholstery. Chair backs were shaped like inverted pears. During the 1850s, these chairs were still relatively undecorated with chair backs outlined by their wooden frames and crowned with a small crest of carved roses. By the 1860s, the carved flowers covered the wooden frame and sometimes *became* the wooden frame.

The structure of chair seats also changed in the middle of the century. During the American Empire period and before, layers of kapok, hair, or matting formed a solid mat under the upholstery. During the mid-century, spiral innerspring seats were invented, creating real comfort for the first time in furniture history. Their use makes Rococo Revival furniture instantly distinguishable from 18th-century Rococo. Rococo *fauteuils* and *bergères* were light and elegant. Rococo Revival equivalents were thick and substantial comfy chairs poised on tiny little wheels.

The other parlor furniture consisted of a center table with cabriole legs and a white marble top, along with several other marble-topped tables for displaying lamps and bibelots and for working. The tables were invariably covered with decorative

Étagère for displaying objets d' arts.

scarves, often more than one layer, including lace doilies under individual objects. Between two windows, a console table with two cabriole legs, a marble top, and a mirror above might be attached to the wall.

Console table.

Another kind of furniture that existed at this time was called bentwood. To modern eyes, bentwood furniture suggests ice cream parlors and cafés. In fact, it was developed in the 1850s and remained popular for utilitarian applications into the 20th century. Chairs, rockers, settees, hat racks, umbrella stands, and tables were all easily available at low cost.

Bentwood rocker.

UPHOLSTERY

The light, clean colors of the Rococo Revival were an important part of the style. The Greek Revival relied heavily on somber black horsehair and scarlet upholstery with lots of gray paintwork. In contrast, the Rococo homemaker wanted feminine, pretty colors and curvy, "elegant" patterns. As though the multiple reverse curves of the furniture weren't enough, the upholstery was most commonly shiny and dull damask figured in Baroque cartouches of foliage and flowers. Pure, intense, pale pastels such as baby blue, pink, and yellow were made possible by the newly developed aniline dyes and were used for upholstery and draperies.

MANTELS

The mantelpiece in a Rococo Revival parlor was almost invariably Italianate. Usually made of white marble, the mantel included a semicircular arched opening and acanthus leaf ornamented consoles sup-

Mantel combining an Italianate shape with Rococo ornament.

China mantel clock in the French taste.

porting the mantel shelf. During the 1860s, before the Aesthetic Movement, the mantelpiece was most often decorated with a purchased mantel garniture consisting of a matched set of central clock, pair of candlesticks, and pair of statues. This set formed a symmetrical arrangement on the cloth that covered the mantel shelf.

FLOORS

Visualize the parlor set with its dark, wooden curves upholstered in pastel damask. Now imagine the floor on which it was perched. Almost certainly it was covered with wall-to-wall carpet. The ingrain of the American Empire style was now old-fashioned and cheap. The arty, oriental rug was still a fashion of the future. The floor of the Rococo Revival parlor was ideally covered in French-style, Aubusson carpet. Napoléon III's accession to the throne in the 1850s promoted a boom in carpetmaking in France. The monarch's patronage supported a new style with large roses and arabesques predominating. By the 1860s, huge roses in dusty pinks, creamy beiges, and soft greens were scattered across the floor.

Aubusson style carpet strewn with roses.

In Devonshire, England, Axminster had long been a center for making luxurious hand-knotted carpets, in imitation of which Halajon Skinner built his first spool loom in 1860. He created a machine-made weave that he called Axminster. This new industrialized process for carpetmaking made rugs less expensive and more accessible. At the time, the ideal carpet pattern was a central figure of dozens of roses surrounded by wreaths and garlands intertwined with Baroque-style moldings and acanthus leaves. There were, of course, variations. The background might be dark-rose, mossy green, or even brown or black. The flowers might be smaller or might be arranged more regularly.

Budget constraints or the limitations of available technology in isolated places might require the purchase of an ingrain carpet in a flowery pattern rather than Aubusson, but the intention to create a French, flowery bower underfoot was certainly there.

WALLS AND CEILINGS

In *Wallpapers in Historic Preservation,* Catherine Frangiamore describes Rococo wallpaper:

> *Scrollwork and miniature scenes appeared in profusion in wallpapers of the mid-19th century.*
>
> *There were also patterns for more sober tastes: in the 1850's and 1860's, papers featuring small embossed gold motifs, evenly spaced over gray or off-white grounds were considered very tasteful. Many of these embossed papers were imported from Germany.*

Now that we have the rose-encrusted furniture placed on the rose-bowered carpet, what did the walls behind this scene look like? There were several choices. Wallpaper came to be machine-made in the 1840s and 1850s, and the price dropped precipitously. The French worked hard to beat the British at technological advances in presses and papermaking, and in many ways succeeded. The most popular wallpapers in the United States were French-made or domestically made knockoffs of French wallpapers. Still, we should not confuse the 1850s and 1860s with later decades. During the 1870s and 1880s, even a small cottage was likely to feature wallpaper in almost every room. During the 1840s, few people had any wallpaper at all, and those who did only used it in one or two public rooms. During the Rococo Revival period, plenty of middle-class parlors still had painted walls, but the norm was wallpapered walls.

Americans imported several kinds of wallpaper patterns from France and imitated them here. There are three types that were popular during the American Empire style: the scenic, the stripe-and-flower pattern, and the gathered fabric type. Other French wallpaper patterns were also derived from fabric. The first was much like chintz, covered with large-scale, many-hued roses and ribbons. Except for the limitations of repeats and widths required by the press, no attempt at regularity was made. These papers were hung with top borders of swagged flowers and fabric. By 1855, the firm of Jules De Fossé in Paris was producing rose-patterned papers with exquisitely modeled, painterly flowers. Only a few years later, American wallpaper manufacturers were printing knockoffs for the domestic market.

The second fabric pattern was paper printed to resemble moiré or watered silk with its distinctive irregular markings. In fact, through the middle of the 19th century, many papers were glazed to resemble silk or satin. These were called *lissage* papers, which is French for "satin." Another cloth often imitated in paper was damask. This was the source of the flocked, damask-like wallpaper most often used in 1960s Westerns to signal "Victorian saloon or bordello."

Finally, one of the most characteristic Rococo Revival wallpapers features French peasant scenes such as Marie Antoinette playing a milkmaid. These scenes were drawn in the style of copperplate engravings—fairly large, and separated by meandering vines and flowers. This class of wallpaper imitated *toile de Jouy* fabrics imported from France.

Borders were almost always used in hanging paper in the mid-

19th century. They were usually darker than the papers and were often flocked and sometimes gilded. Wallpapers were cut with shears at this time, and the gaps between the edge of the paper and the woodwork or ceiling had to be neatened up with some kind of border.

During the 1850s, an "architectural" treatment became popular and was used through the Rococo Revival era. Walls were vertically divided into panels by wallpaper frames. These rectangular or lozenge-shaped panels were filled by paint or by wallpaper imitating tufted fabric or damask, or even toile de Jouy. Real moldings were not often used during this period to create wall panels. They belong to the French revivals of the 1880s and 1890s.

According to Catherine Frangiamore:

> By mid-century, the use of borders diminished slightly. They grew narrower, and were for the most part confiined to the tops of walls. But in the 1850's and 1860's a French fashion for dividing the wall into vertical panels, formed by border papers or by wallpaper "pilasters" again focused fashionable attention in wallpaper borders .... These panel decorations, many of which included elaborate dados imitating architectural paneling and carving, were known as "fresco decorations" and required clever handling to be fitted on a wall.

PICTURES AND MIRRORS

To go back to our Rococo Revival parlor, we have the furniture arranged conversationally on the rose-bowered, wall-to-wall carpet. We have walls papered in vertical panels, roses, or Marie Antoinette gamboling with her sheep. We also have mirrors and pictures.

The mirrors are important because they were so revolutionary. The huge, ornamental mirror with gilded frame was a Rococo Revival introduction. From the early 19th century, most glass used for both windows and mirrors was cylinder glass. This means that a glass blower made a large bottle with straight sides. He then cut off the top and bottom and slit the side of the resulting cylinder. The glass relaxed while in a hot oven and flattened out into a rectangular sheet.

This process obviously limited sheets of glass to the size of the largest bottle a man could blow. That's why large Greek Revival ogee mirrors need a wooden muntin to join two pieces of glass.

Rococo Revival over-mantel mirror in gilt gesso.

The French, however, manufactured huge sheets of plate glass by pouring molten glass into zinc-lined trays polished to mirror smoothness. Because they were not constrained by the size of the bubble blown or the size of the oven used to flatten a sheet, they could create huge slabs of plate glass. These sheets were available in the United States only at great cost, since they had to be shipped across the Atlantic and incurred import duties. They were used mostly for commercial storefronts and for mirrors in bars and wealthy houses. To this day, some older people still call large sheets of glass, French plate glass. Because of this advance in technology pioneered in the 1840s in France and imitated in the 1850s in the United States, the overmantel mirror in a Rococo Revival parlor could reach from the mantel shelf to the ceiling. The mirror frame was most likely to be gilded gesso with swirling arabesques culminating in a large central cartouche that projected in front of the room cornice. By the 1850s, America was manufacturing its own plate glass, and even middle-class parlors could boast a Versaillesesque looking glass. Because plate glass was associated with France, large plate-glass mirrors seemed especially appropriate for French-style interiors.

The family portraits that would have graced the American Empire parlor were now gone, perhaps because they reminded everyone of humble origins. Instead, there were copies of Raphael and Watteau for the middle class and oil paintings in Baroque and Rococo styles for the wealthy. Also popular were engravings and lithographs of famous landscapes, allegorical subjects, scenes of classical antiquity, or sacred and profane love, often produced by "high-minded" academic artists whose names have since been forgotten. Genre scenes of European peasantry behaving picturesquely seem to have been favorites.

Just beginning was the fashion for the Victorian story picture that remained popular for the rest of the century. A young woman receiving a love note from her banished swain, a child shedding a tear over a broken flowerpot, a noble St. Bernard standing proudly in the snow with his lifesaving keg of brandy—all of these and hundreds more formed the favorite pictorial subjects of middle-class, mid-century homes. Photographs became widely available in the 1860s, and family portraits or tintypes of soldiers serving in the Civil War were often seen. Photos of naked two-year-olds as cupid with bow and arrow enjoyed enormous success.

"There He Is" engraving by Thomas Nast is an example of popular Victorian story pictures.

Picture frames that were vertical rectangles with shallow, arched tops first made their appearance during the 1850s and 1860s in the Italianate and Rococo style. Elaborately curved gilt, gesso frames in Rococo style were popular during the 1860s, following the lead of the mirror frames. The matting of photos was still relatively simple as the era of asymmetrical, wildly gathered, and pleated mats was still to come in the 1880s. Frames would be hung at eye level, tilted down perhaps more than modern people do, and sometimes still blind hung (with no cords showing). This is when hanging pictures with long cords from a picture molding or picture pin was introduced.

LIGHTING

Illuminating gas was first made available in the United States in Baltimore in the 1820s. It then became more widely available in major cities such as Philadelphia and New York. During the 1830s and by the 1850s and 1860s, it was common even in small towns. The first kind of gas developed was bituminous coal gas. This got a big boost when coal was exploited in Pennsylvania in the 1850s. After 1872, coal gas was replaced by "water gas," which was supplanted by natural gas in modern times. Most gas burners after 1876 were either flat flame jets or they worked on the Argand principle.

Kerosene was invented in 1854 as a refinement of petroleum (along with a useless by-product called gasoline). Kerosene burned brighter than most oil and was inexpensive. It revolutionized lighting and enabled people to stay up into the evening. There are numerous names for different kinds of kerosene lamps but they fall into several simple categories just like oil lamps: single wick, duplex (two wicks), sineumbra, and Argand. The first kerosene lamps used a single flat wick raised by a thumbscrew. In 1865, a duplex burner with two parallel, flat wicks about an eighth of an inch apart was introduced. In 1888, an improved central draft burner (much like the Argand) was

Argand gas burner.

Fishtail or flat-flame jet gas burner.

introduced by Henry E. Schaffer, who called it the Rochester Burner. The "student lamp" was patented in 1871 by A. M. Blake and consisted of a lamp with a detachable font in an arm opposite the burner. It was also called the "Harvard lamp" after the university that ordered them for their dormitories. And still people used burning fluid or camphene lamps in the 1850s, though their pesky habit of exploding and burning down the house did give them a bad name. Fire insurance companies charged extra if aware of their use.

In the parlor, a gasolier would be hung from the center of the ceiling. The 1850s and 1860s parlor gasolier consisted of a single tier of four, five, or six burners on curved, cast-brass arms radiating from a central supply pipe. Ornamental chains might swag from the central pipe to the burners. The shades were likely to be plain globes with lightly acid-etched designs. The heavily faceted bowls or cone-shaped shades we associate with Victoriana mostly belong to later decades.

There is an interesting evolution in the design of Rococo Revival gasoliers. The 1850s examples all show a single tier of burners either with a central pipe or with rods or pipes to each burner. In the 1860s and later, there might be two or three tiers of burners always with a central supply pipe. The 1850s gasoliers show a fashion for surrounding the central stem with small statues of allegorical figures, while the later ones use many hanging, faceted prisms. We should also remember that during the 1850s and 1860s, there were a large number of cast-iron gasoliers made. Especially for middle-class rather than wealthy homes, cast-iron gasoliers and kerosene chandeliers were an appropriate choice.

This Rococo Revival gasolier shows the cast, curved arms characteristic of the style.

Besides the central, pendant fixture in the room, matching wall sconces often flanked the mantel. Sometimes additional sconces might be installed where they would illuminate a mirror or a desk, though this practice was more common in rooms other than the parlor.

There were numerous lamps in the Victorian parlor. During the 1850s, the most common was still the oil lamp, now often molded all in glass with its inverted pear-shaped font perfect for Rococo decoration. These lamps were fairly small and were furnished with dome-shaped shades for reading, or globe-shaped shades for general tasks, or no shades at all. A common mistake in showing period rooms is to display the lamps on tables and desks throughout the day. In fact, throughout the 19th century the lamps were gathered up in the morning to be refilled, have the wicks trimmed, the chimneys cleaned, and to be redistributed around the house in the evening. A lamp with a full font is much safer than a half-filled one because there is less room for vapors to accumulate and, perhaps, explode.

Gas table lamp fed by a rubber tube.

Gas table lamps fed by a rubber tube from a gasolier or sconce appeared as early as 1853 and persisted through the rest of the century. They were never very popular though, and the pattern of fixed lighting in gas and moveable lamps in kerosene was much more common. Another solution to the problem of providing reading light was to include a central lyre or harp lamp as part of a gasolier. This lamp could be lowered over a central table and was furnished with a dome-shaped shade to reflect light downward. The glass and crystal chandelier that we most associate with the Victorian era is really a part of the 1860s Rococo Revival that persisted as the French style for the rest of the century.

WINDOWS

The Rococo Revival style really marks the end of restraint in window decorations. In the preceding period, even middle-class people might have only a bug bar to keep out flies and a window shade or venetian blind to keep out the sun.

During the mid-century Rococo Revival, no self-respecting window had less than five parts to the décor. Above the window, a cornice topped the whole arrangement. It might be made of gessoed and gilded wood moldings but was most likely to be thin, pressed metal in Rococo swirls. The tiebacks were often made of pressed metal to match. Hanging below the cornice was a valance or pelmet. This was usually a solid color with a figure in shiny and matte finish like damask or moiré silk. The valance could be gathered into swags and jabots and ornamented with wide braid sewn on the surface near the edge, with deep fringe and swags of cording and tassels hanging from strategic points. Alternatively, the pelmet might be flat and stiff with a Rococo style silhouette cut out and bordered in braid and fringe. The drapes themselves most often matched the fabric of the valance and were very full and gathered into large folds. They would be held open by cord and tassel tiebacks or by metal tiebacks positioned low on the drapes to modern eyes. In a luxurious setting, the drapes might also puddle on the floor in a decorative arrangement. Velvets, silks, satins, wool rep, and other heavy plush fabrics were considered appropriate in parlors. The color usually matched the upholstery, the walls, or both, as upholstering *en-suite* was still the classy thing to do. This was before the cult of self-expression made artistic mismatching de rigueur.

Rococo Revival window treatment with pressed metal cornice.

Flowery lace window curtains were introduced in the mid-19th century.

Under the drapes was another set of lighter curtains made of lace or net. These, too, would be drawn back to expose a sash-curtain or window shade. Window shades were still raised by strings in the 1860s. The spring variety that we use today was invented in the 1880s. The material of the shade was linen—printed, painted, or stenciled with a conventionalized flower border or with a romantic landscape scene. Special papers featuring romantic scenery were called curtain papers and were printed to be used on window shades.

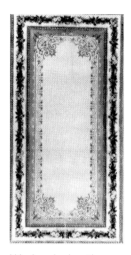

Window shade with Rococo decoration.

BEDROOM

The Rococo Revival bedroom was quite a grand affair compared with its predecessors. First, the bed was likely to feature a huge, arched, rosewood headboard with a ruffle of carved roses at its upper edge. The footboard was a smaller version without the carving. In some great ones, especially by Belter, the whole bed is curved in plan with the headboard and footboard wrapping around the mattress, and the high sideboards undulating their way between. These beds give a whole new meaning to "getting *into* bed," since it feels like boarding a boat, not going to sleep.

John Henry Belter bed.

In the Rococo Revival style, the rest of the bedroom furniture was likely, much more than before, to be part of a matched set. The armoire repeated the shape and carving of the bed, the chest of drawers usually featured a mirror with a similarly arched and rose-bowered top, and chairs, tables, and commode (bedside cabinet for the chamber pot) completed the scene.

The walls were often papered in a stripe-and-flower French or French-style wallpaper and the trim painted warm white. The floor would be carpeted in light colored wall-to-wall ingrain or, in a wealthy house, Axminster or Aubusson-like Belgian carpet. The pattern was almost assuredly roses—moderate size in the 1850s, huge in the 1860s, and back to moderate in the 1870s. The upholstery, curtains, and bed hangings were usually a printed cotton like *toile de Jouy* or chintz. However, the practice of matching the wallpaper and fabrics in a room did not exist.

Lighting in the mid-century bedroom often included a gas sconce. Jointed, flexible wall lights were often used to get light near mirrors during the 1850s. Small kerosene or oil lamps were traditionally set out on a tray in the hallway for people to light and take to their bedrooms. These lamps generally featured a finger hole to make them safe to carry while lighted.

Rococo Revival dresser with curved drawers and applied roses.

Rococo Revival gas sconce.

FRENCH STYLE: 1880s–1890s

O nce introduced, the Rococo Revival hung on to popularity year after year. Fashionable women chose the elegance of *tout les Louis* from the 1850s well into the 20th century. The Louis XVI and Marie Antoinette styles clung to life with a tenacity that might well have been envied by the royal couple themselves. In each decade, however, America's romance with 18th-century French design took different forms. Although 1860s Rococo Revival, 1880s and 1890s French style, 1900s Edith Wharton French, 1960s French Provincial, and 1970s and 1980s Pierre Deux Country French were all inspired by 18th-century France, they were all different from each other, and they all displayed the "look" of their own time.

By the 1890s, Rococo swirls were glued onto "golden oak" furniture in many bedroom suites manufactured in Grand Rapids, Michigan. Lots of massive oak tables had at least rudimentary cabriole legs, and probably most china, clocks, silverware, and objets d'art displayed the roses and curlicues of the "French taste." Compared with the 1860s, when the Rococo Revival was a style favored by the wealthy, the 1880s and 1890s saw its dissemination down the social ladder to working-class interiors. French design also split in the 1890s between the wealthy, ultra-refined Marie Antoinette and the working-class, solid, golden oak strains.

Oak furniture often had composition ornament glued onto otherwise plain furniture.

About 1900, there was a clear turning away from the eclecticism and clutter of the Victorian interior. Edith Wharton and Ogden Codman, Jr., popularized a light-filled, restrained style. Pictures were no longer to be hung at odd angles from long cords, as they had been since the end of the Greek Revival era. No more dark varnished wood-work and piles of knickknacks. No more muddy or strident colors. No more elaborate drapes and fussy *passementeries*. Everything was to be ivory with restrained gilding. The Victorian era was finally dead. What was this new style? Rococo, of course, specifically Marie Antoinette. It is extraordinary how quickly she revived as the first 20th-century style after being laid to rest as the last Victorian.

FURNITURE

The era of the wildest Rococo furniture was over by the 1870s. However, even though the style was waning, most Victorian ladies still chose French furniture and rejected the Aesthetic Movement as too inelegant. In the 1870s and 1880s, there was a definite turn to the Louis XVI style with its tapered, fluted legs instead of cabriole legs. In a thoroughly Louis XVI-style chair, the chair back was a wooden, oval frame filled with tufted upholstery. In fact, the fashion for Louis XVI penetrated the Aesthetic Movement to such an extent that *most* chairs that are otherwise Eastlake feature Louis XVI legs.

Louis XVI style settee.

Left: An otherwise Aesthetic Movement chair still might have Louis XVI legs. Right: Louis XVI legs on a modest drop leaf table.

During the 1890s, an extra feminine version of the French Style developed called Marie Antoinette, featuring furniture that was especially light in proportion, often with painted frames highlighted with gilding and ivory-colored silk damask upholstery. It still had the

This Marie Antoinette style parlor shows the delicate ivory painted furniture and pale silk upholstery that are hallmarks of the style.

This late 19th-century French-style wallpaper has a frieze and field arrangement worked out in roses.

thick, innerspring seats and casters to distinguish it from real 18th-century furniture. It also mixed with abandon Rococo curves and more classical Louis XVI elements. However, Marie Antoinette furniture was more like its 18th-century models than other Victorian French furniture.

WALLS AND CEILINGS

People furnishing French-style parlors in the 1890s began to create Rococo wall panels using moldings. During the 1850s and 1860s, vertical wall panels with curved corners or tops were often formed by using wallpaper. By the 1890s, the moldings outlining the panels were no longer made of paper, but were actual three-dimensional moldings. As before, the panels might be filled with wallpaper that was flocked in the pattern of damask or looked like *toile de Jouy*. The preferred color schemes were pretty sharp—red, blue, or green with white backgrounds.

LIGHTING

Two kinds of lamps were introduced in the late 19th-century French style. One is the so-called Gone with the Wind Lamp. It consisted of a large glass globe, with a concealed kerosene reservoir inside, supporting a large, glass, globe-shaped shade. The font and shade were colored and painted to match, usually with overblown roses. The other new lamp in the 1890s was the "banquet lamp." It had a 15-to-18-inch-tall base made of cast grillwork supporting a kerosene font and was used as a table lamp and on sideboards, as well as in other places.

Banquet lamp.

In gaslighting, two developments during this era were applied to lamps of every style. First, in 1885, Robert William Von Bunsen invented the Bunsen burner, which mixed air and gas together. Second, Welsbach introduced the Welsbach mantle in 1887. It was a little cotton bag soaked in thorium and ceria which glowed when held over a Bunsen burner. This gave an extraordinarily bright light compared to the exposed flames that preceded it. Before the Welsbach mantle, a gasolier produced six to eight candlepower per burner. With the Welsbach mantle, each burner produced 20 candlepower. In 1897, Welsbach introduced a downward-facing mantle to compete with the new downward-facing electric lights.

This parlor features paneled walls, elaborate plaster ceiling decorations, pale damask upholstery, a Rococo mantel with a huge gilt overmantel, and an Aubusson rug.

ITALIANATE: 1860S

For those mid-century people who looked for an alternative to the Rococo Revival—something grand rather than pretty—there was always the Italianate. To Victorians, the Italianate style was a mixed revival of Renaissance and Baroque motifs, relying heavily on architectural effects rather than ephemeral flower patterns. In the same way that 19th-century folk recombined historic motifs in the Gothic Revival style and relied on easy cues to identify things (for example, the pointed arch), Victorians took the bracketed cornice as the hallmark of the Italianate style.

Classical consoles support a cornice.

The Italianate style is the mid-19th-century way of expressing solid, middle-class confidence in the progress of civilization, education, and Western culture. First generation members of the middle class, who wanted to emphasize that they were a part of the great European tradition of art and letters, built in the Italianate style. Schools, city halls, and men's clubs were often built as palazzi with heavy, bracketed cornices. Houses for beer barons and machine-tool magnates proclaimed solid respectability from their rusticated basements to their cupolas.

The interiors of most Italianate houses were furnished in French Rococo Revival style, but some, especially when the desired effect was substantial, grand, even magnificent, were Italianate. Often the architectural framework of an interior was Italianate and the furnishings mixed Italianate and Rococo.

FURNITURE

There never was a lot of mid-19th-century Italianate furniture. Even rarer was a whole interior in this style. Instead, predominately Ro-

coco Revival interiors included some Italianate
furniture where it was thought appropriate. In
the library, for instance, bookcases might feature
architectural-looking cornices and pilasters. A
sideboard or storage cabinet, which is sort of
palazzo-shaped anyway, might include segmental-
arched panels in its doors with a heavy cornice supporting the top.

Italianate bed.

Another complication in picturing mid-19th-century Italianate
furniture is that this style develops into the late 19th-century Renaissance Revival. Even though the fashion for the Italian Renaissance of
the 1850s and 1860s waned in the 1870s and early 1880s in favor of
Gothicism and the Aesthetic Movement in its many forms, the style
reasserted itself by the middle of the 1880s as Renaissance Revival.
There is no break between mid-century Italianate style and 1880s
Renaissance Revival. Instead, there is a continuum of furniture inspired
by Renaissance and Baroque architecture. However, the massively
corniced beds, parlor sets, dressers, and tables featuring cartouches
and women's faces definitely belong to the late 19th century.

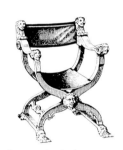

Savonarola chair.

WALLS AND CEILINGS

Along with the bracketed cornice, other features of the Italianate style
include segmentally arched window and door openings, broad deep
casings, and baseboards consisting of cyma recta (S-curve) and fillet
moldings. The ceiling of a parlor, dining room, or hall usually featured
a central medallion from which the gasolier hung. The medallion was
often composed of conventionalized acanthus leaves or classical moldings with Renaissance enrichments of waterleaf, bead and reel, and

Simple Italianate armoire.

egg and dart. The meeting of the ceiling and the wall displayed the cornice. In any house with pretensions to magnificence, the cornice in the parlors was made up of premolded modillions ornamenting a full display of classical moldings. In a simple cottage, the cornice could consist of run-in-place moldings with a deep cavetto (cove) or cyma (S-curve) shadow.

Italianate ceiling medallion.

An alternative to the central medallion and cornice arrangement for an Italianate room is the coffered ceiling. This scheme, where the ceiling is divided into boxes by richly ornamented moldings, was certainly confined to the interiors of the rich and famous. As the century wore on, coffered ceilings came to be vaguely associated with dining rooms, perhaps implying Renaissance feasting in the ancestral manor house. They never became common in the 19th century, but enjoyed a brief revival in early 20th-century dining rooms. In the early 20th century, oak-beamed or coffered ceilings were intended to imply medieval halls, not Renaissance palazzi.

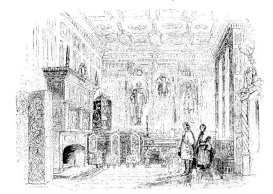

Coffered ceiling.

The walls of an Italianate parlor were most often plain paint, but also might be organized by wallpaper moldings into vertical panels with curved corners. When the walls were divided into panels by these trompe l'oeil paper moldings, the color was usually stone: limestone, sand, or putty. A paper molding chair rail and dado panels might also complete the scheme.

Italianate mantel.

MANTELS

As with all Victorian styles, the focal point of the parlor is the fireplace. An Italianate fireplace was usually a marble arch with a marble mantel shelf. The opening might be fitted with a cast-iron insert to burn coal as the mid-19th century was the boom period for coal heat. Above the mantel shelf, a large mirror in a gilded frame topped the ensemble.

FLOORS

The Italianate floor was covered by wall-to-wall carpet. The archetypal pattern consisted of bits of architecture—cornices, cartouches, acanthus leaves—forming a large central medallion with roses or vines interspersed. Of course, since most interiors were mixed style, Baroque C-curves and Rococo Revival roses were often included in the same carpet.

WINDOWS

The standard Italianate door or window is segmentally arched; that is, the top is curved, but less than a half-circle. (The arch is made of only a segment of a circle, hence the name.)

Window treatments, as in many styles during the second half of the 19th century, were heavy and elaborate. The many layered, gathered, and swagged draperies that were introduced in the Rococo Revival of the 1850s and 1860s persisted through almost every other style. Even in interiors that were otherwise Italianate, Aesthetic, Gothic, or Queen Anne, the curtains were as likely to be elaborately gathered, fringed, and tasseled as the most French of parlors. There were other, simpler, window treatments, but the French version became the middle-class idea of *luxe* and was used in the unlikeliest settings.

This hall features segmentally arched doors and elaborate Rococo Revival toile de Jouy wallpaper.

GOTHIC REVIVAL: 1845–1850S

The Gothic Revival was a part of the Romantic Movement, which promoted the view that long ago and far away were infinitely better than here and now. The long ago was frequently the Middle Ages and the far away could be exotic cultures or the untamed wilderness. Natural was, by definition, good. And orderly, symmetrical, classical, and civilized were, by definition, bad. The Romantic Movement provided a set of assumptions for the Gothic Revival, the Aesthetic Movement, the Queen Anne, and the Arts and Crafts styles.

The Gothic Revival style contained a clear message: it proclaimed the simple, honest heritage of the English yeoman. The romantic asymmetry of the Cottage Gothic was contrasted in the Victorian's mind with the classical pretensions of the Greek Revival style that reeked of Napoléon's revolution and dictatorship. For a long time, the Gothic was considered to be *the* peculiarly English style. It did not matter that the style was invented at St. Dénis by the Abbé Suger. Chartres and Nôtre Dame de Paris did not count. The quaintness and irregular massing of the Gothic style were so much in keeping with the English love of eccentricity, their rejection of systematization in favor of tradition, precedent, and local customs, that

An Andrew Jackson Downing Gothic cottage.

Americans believed that the Gothic Revival embodied all that was valuable in the Anglo-Saxon tradition.

Alexander Jackson Davis and Andrew Jackson Downing first popularized the Gothic Revival style in America during the 1840s. They promoted it as more "natural" than the Greek Revival and so more suitable for country residences (though it's hard to see how a build-

ing in any style can be "natural"). This
early version of the Gothic Revival is
often called Carpenter Gothic or
Cottage Gothic. These buildings were
considered Gothic because they featured pointed windows and asymmetrical massing. In no way were they
archeologically correct revivals of real
Gothic forms.

In fact, real Gothic houses had
been small and likely to be wattle and
daub, half-timbered, mud, or stick huts with none of the church decoration we associate with the name Gothic. Later in the 19th century,
during the period we call High Victorian Gothic, architects studied
medieval church architecture (not houses) and applied those Gothic
designs to grand houses and public buildings.

*Gothic Revival cottage
designed by Alexander
Jackson Davis.*

FURNITURE

In fact, Americans had absolutely no idea what the interiors and furniture from the Middle Ages looked like. Real Gothic furniture resembled packing crates, boards, and sawhorses that followed their
owners from castle to castle. Instead of copying these, Americans took
the same forms that were used for American Empire furniture and
added a little decoration taken from the tracery of cathedral
windows. An otherwise Empire, mahogany-veneered bedstead might
have a headboard composed of three flamboyant Gothic arches. The
usual eared Ionic back of a side chair might be replaced with a pointed

Gothic Revival chair.

Downing's design for a simple Gothic bookcase.

Downing showed how to make Gothic ceilings out of simple moldings.

Downing combined ceilings with false beams, pointed arches in doorways, and pointed mirrors and chairs for a Gothic parlor.

arch and, thereby, become Gothic. Bookcases could have pointed arch, glass doors. The central column of a pedestal table might be replaced with clustered columns or crocketed buttresses.

During the mid-century Gothic Revival, the practice of displaying curiosities in Victorian parlors began. J.C. Loudon, in the *Encyclopedia of Cottage, Farm and Villa Architecture,* recommended busts and sculpture for the well-to-do, and stones, ores, minerals, books, and objects of art and antiquity as decoration for the more modest parlor. From paintings and illustrations of the time in Edgar Mayhew's *A Documentary History of American Interiors,* it is clear that the objects in the parlor were still displayed in moderation with none of the wild excess of the 1870s and 1880s.

WALLS AND CEILINGS

Catherine Frangiamore writes that "using wallpaper, the Gothic Revival found its way into numerous domestic interiors during the 1840's and 1850's, while in many cases exteriors remained chastely classical. During this period, combinations of vivid green with gray, strong harsh red with brown, or a brilliant shade of blue paired with brown were particularly popular."

Walls in the early phase of the Gothic Revival were almost invariably plain paint, no different from the Greek Revival style. Andrew Jackson Downing advised that the trim color should never match the predominant wall color in a room. Also, white paint was never appropriate, in Downing's view, for use in country residences because it was unnatural. He grudgingly allowed that it might be acceptable in a city drawing room, since that venue was so unnatural anyway. Unlike the more colorful wallpapers, the most common interior colors for painted walls were probably putty, dove, gray, and sand, just as for exteriors. Some Gothic Revivalists recommended colors that anticipated the Aesthetic colors of the 1870s and 1880s, such as sage and "fallen leaf" (brown).

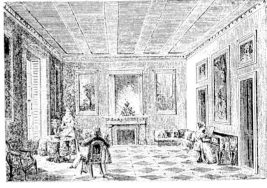

The diaper-patterned carpet introduced in the 1840s remained popular for decades.

In the 1840s, Downing included several drawings of Gothic style rooms in *The Architecture of Country Houses.* He favored ceilings with false beams made of attached three-quarter round moldings as a Gothic alternative to the cornices and medallions found in classical houses. Sometimes the beams were crossed in both directions to form coffers. At each intersection a small wooden boss covered the joint. In high-style Gothic Revival interiors, the ceiling could be decorated with fan vaulting or strapwork, though this was confined to wealthy villas and mansions.

This kind of Gothic trompe l'oeil wallpaper became fashionable during the 1840s.

FLOORS

Downing, along with Alexander Jackson Davis, introduced a novelty in floors that became popular. By staining alternate floorboards dark, a decorative effect could be achieved with almost no investment. Carpets with diaper patterning, that is, patterns whose alternate rows are set-off a half-step, also became fashionable. These diamond-shaped, lozenge patterns stayed popular through all the Gothic styles of the 19th century.

LIGHTING

In the Gothic Revival, as well as in its contemporary style, American Empire, people still used candles and oil lamps. Candles were expensive and candlesticks were seldom the highly decorated dining table accoutrements we see today. Some Gothic-inspired, molded glass candlesticks were made, but it is unlikely that many people worried about coordinating the style of the candlesticks and the interior.

Spiky Gothic gasolier.

Oil lamps usually featured an upside-down, pear-shaped and pear-sized font supported by a metal column or figurine standing on a square, marble base. Again, there were Gothic-style versions made, but it is unlikely that anyone worried about consistent style. When the kerosene lamp and the gasolier became common after mid-century, many of them featured Gothic elements. Though no different in structure from their Rococo contemporaries, Gothic kerosene lamps could feature trefoil and quatrefoil ornament cast onto the base, and romantic scenes of castles and abbeys painted on the shades.

Gothic gasoliers tended to have straight or jagged arms as opposed to the S-curve of the Rococo Revival. When the arms were irregular, they were likely to be made of cast metal rather than extruded brass pipe, which was more suitable for curves. The standard ornaments were trefoils and quatrefoils, coats of arms, and conventionalized flowers.

WINDOWS

Pointed Gothic casement windows crowned by a label lintel.

It is unlikely that very many Carpenter Gothic interiors extended the style to the window decorations. Of course, pointed windows are inherently Gothic and don't need Gothic drapes for style. In his book, Downing shows Greek and Gothic lambrequins, which are both flat pieces of cloth suspended from a wooden cornice box. In the Greek version, the lambrequin is horizontal, and in the Gothic, the bottom edge is cut to form a shallow, pointed arch.

Another lambrequin that was considered Gothic and was used from the 1840s through the rest of the century was the Van Dyck. Imagine the castellated top of a medieval fortress with its alternating solids and slots. Now turn that upside down and make the bottom edge of each hanging "flag" slightly pointed. That is a Van Dyck lambrequin. They were used above windows, on mantels, and as table scarves and portières.

A third Gothic treatment, which was rare at mid-century and became more popular with later versions of the Gothic Revival, is the curtain rod as medieval lance. An exposed iron or brass rod with a cast spear point as finial could add a Gothic touch to any window or door opening. This approach was seldom used, however, until the Aesthetic Movement Gothic became popular in the 1870s and 1880s.

A new invention in mid-century America was the painted roller-blind. These cloth window shades with painted scenes of picturesque ruins or castles became popular in the Gothic style of the 1840s and 1850s. Shades like these were found in every Victorian style with conventionalized borders, bucolic French scenes, or classical ornament available to suit the style of individual parlors. Special papers, called curtain papers, were also printed just for use on roller-blinds.

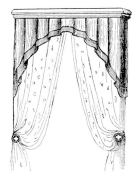

Gothic window treatment.

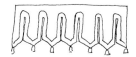

Van Dyck lambrequin.

Romantic scene from a Gothic window shade.

HIGH VICTORIAN GOTHIC: 1860S–1870S

The Carpenter Gothic of the 1840s and 1850s developed into the High Victorian Gothic of the 1860s and 1870s. The High Victorian Gothic was much more "correct" than its predecessor, though not as "correct" as the early 20th-century Gothic that followed it. In many buildings, the High Victorian Gothic was most characterized by colors inherent in the building materials—different color roof slates to create diaper patterns, different color bricks to pattern wall surfaces, or brown sandstone and granite to stripe arches. The High Victorian Gothic was much more likely to be used for churches, schools, and market buildings than for houses. When it was used for residential interiors, it had the same degree of elaborateness as its contemporary style, the Rococo Revival.

Gothic chairs in a High Victorian Gothic hall.

WALLS AND CEILINGS

A High Victorian Gothic ceiling might feature a central ceiling medallion and cornice just like an Italianate or Rococo Revival interior. The ceiling medallion frequently included trefoils or quatrefoils and resembled the tracery of a rose window on a medieval cathedral. The cornice often used three-quarter round or cusped moldings with crockets or shallow pointed arches incorporated for a Gothic effect. In a high-style, custom-made interior, strapwork divided the ceiling into elaborate compartments. This kind of decoration really looked more like German Baroque ornament, though it might be related to plate tracery in Gothic windows.

By the middle of the 19th century, numerous wallpaper patterns featured Gothic themes. The 1850s saw the introduction of papers with scenes of castles glimpsed through foliage. In fact, wallpapers where small landscape scenes were rigidly ordered into columns and rows already existed. Now they were replaced by papers featuring larger scenes separated by and seen through meandering foliage.

In the latter third of the 19th century, wall surfaces changed with the introduction of two new products—

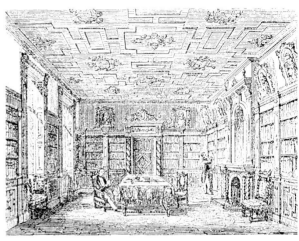

Strapwork ceiling.

Lincrusta and Anaglypta. Lincrusta was invented by Frederick Walton during the 1870s in England. It was a material about halfway between cardboard and linoleum, consisting of paper and linseed oil. The steel rollers that produced it could mold the material into high relief. After it was pasted on the walls, it was painted, glazed, and varnished to emphasize the design and to create a tough, waterproof surface. Gothic tracery, Rococo swirls, Italianate coffers, Aesthetic diaper designs, even Art Nouveau whiplashes and Colonial Revival swags and urns were produced in this miracle material. It was the vinyl wood paneling or Formica of its day and was often used in high-traffic areas such as vestibules, halls, and stairways.

Anaglypta was the poor cousin of Lincrusta, consisting of heavily embossed cardboard without the linseed oil. It was also painted, glazed, and varnished. Both of these materials were often finished to resemble tooled leather with dark glazes and gilded highlights.

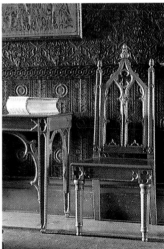

An ecclesiastically Gothic chair and table in front of Lincrusta walls.

THE AESTHETIC MOVEMENT: 1875–1880S

The Aesthetic Movement differs from previous eras in interior decoration in that it is not a style—it is a movement, an ethic, an attitude. In the middle of the 19th century in England, an extreme reaction began against the materialism of the Industrial Revolution. No one really doubted that the Industrial Revolution gave more people a better life than ever before. But many things were lost in the all-conquering, mechanical march toward progress. Before the Industrial Revolution, families worked together on family farms. After the revolution, individuals were employees working in factories and living in tenements. Before the revolution, consumer goods were scarce, but those that existed were handmade and meant to be passed down as heirlooms. After the revolution, objects became plentiful, but they changed—silver became silver plate, mouth-blown glass became molded glass, and tapestry wall-hangings became off-the-rack wallpaper.

The Aesthetic Movement included several styles and many, often conflicting, philosophies. But they all had a number of aspects in common. All of these aesthetes believed that aesthetics, that is, beauty rather than ugliness, meant something more than just appearance. They believed that beauty was more honest, true, and good than ugliness, and that the goodness of beauty had a moral effect on the world. They also idealized the handmade and the artist. The familiar myth of the driven artist starving in a garret being more noble in spirit than the richest aristocrat is a Victorian invention. This fevered worshipping of "genius," this separating the artist from the common herd of humanity, was one of the hallmarks of the Aesthetic Movement.

The most famous writer of the Aesthetic Movement was John

Ruskin. He exalted the artist above all others and fervently insisted on the uplifting role of aesthetics in life. Ruskin also cemented the association of Gothic architecture with the Aesthetic Movement. Most aesthetes used Gothic architecture as their illustration of how structure can be honestly expressed in architectural form, and how ornament can develop naturally out of the practical shapes in the building.

Oddly enough, Ruskin's particular fetish was Venetian Gothic architecture, probably the least structural and organic version ever. Venetians just had more money than anyone else in Europe when International Gothic was at its height. They frosted their palazzi with an icing of Gothic tracery to update otherwise traditional buildings.

Ruskin was also the leader of one of the two factions into which the Aesthetic Movement split. Charles Locke Eastlake and his friends who founded the South Kensington School in London formed the other side of the controversy. Eastlake and the others railed against the trompe l'oeil effects that were so common in the middle-class taste of their time: perspective used in the design of house decorations to create the illusion of depth in flat surfaces; wallpapers with scenes or even shaded, three-dimensional-looking roses; carpets with roses and rococo moldings scattered across the design; printed *toile de Jouy* fabrics with scenes of pre-Revolutionary, French shepherdesses in sylvan glades. All these were condemned by Eastlake and friends as dishonest because they dealt in the *illusion* of three dimen-

This 1880s advertisement shows an Aesthetic interior with portières divided into dado, field, and frieze, artfully arranged overmantel shelves, and exposed wood floor with area rug.

sions. Because they were dishonest, they were ugly and an evil force in the world leading to the degradation of morals in modern life.

Ruskin would have none of this. He so exalted the creative impulse that he would have no rules limit the artist's choice. He ridiculed the two-dimensional, heraldic-looking patterns that the Eastlake camp prescribed by comparing them unfavorably to the great murals found in Italian palazzi. He claimed that all great art was inspired by nature, and that no conventionalized creation of "compass and rule" could ever compete with the wonders of flowers.

An Eastlake chair with Egyptian lotus blossoms in the crest, an Anglo-Japanese table, and an Eastlake bookcase all sit on an Oriental carpet.

So two camps formed, both agreeing on the depravity of modern (Victorian) life and morals, and both prescribing better aesthetics to remedy the problem. Unfortunately, the two camps gave opposite advice on how to judge what was beautiful. On the whole, the Eastlake side won the hearts and minds of the aesthetes because their two-dimensional designs and particular proportions and colors were identifiable. Ruskin's style differed from the middle-class, poor taste that he deplored more in quality than in style, and quality is notoriously difficult to pin down.

In 1889 a woman named Eliza M. Lavin wrote a book called *Home-Making and House Keeping*. Her book gave detailed advice on furnishing and decorating homes for various income levels. The advice was not daring or innovative or particularly up-to-date. Rather, it was extremely conventional and gives us a good picture of what people of the time considered proper and appropriate in different conditions. First, she describes a cottage. Since it is a workingman's home, the interior trim is to be pine, stained, and shellacked to look like walnut. Carpets throughout the home are oriental in design with ingrain in the bedrooms (very inexpensive in the 1880s), and an "Agra" in the public rooms downstairs. Presumably an "Agra" is an Axminster or Wilton loomed, machine-made, oriental carpet. In the bedroom, the walls are papered with a chintz-like pattern. Various bedrooms have matched suites of furniture in walnut, ash, and maple, and one bedroom features a brass bed. None of the upstairs furniture is upholstered, though rockers in the bedrooms do have seat cushions.

Eliza Lavin's book makes it clear that ordinary householders were not obsessed with consistency. Lavin's houses mixed the prettiness of French-style furniture with exotic touches from Japan and the Middle East. By the late 1880s, the Aesthetic Movement had been around long enough that its original intention was long forgotten, and it became just another repertoire of decorative motifs.

Lavin goes on to describe a "better sort of house" (meaning middle-class rather than working-class). She skips describing all-olive-green color schemes because of their ubiquitousness and recommends olive, terra-cotta, and warm, pinkish gray with off-white trim as an appropriate scheme for a middle-class house. Olive green color schemes were, by far, the most popular choice for Aesthetic Movement devotees. Lavin confirms this by trying to discourage their use: "They have not been mentioned in the schemes of color thus far introduced, because they are too often permitted on account of their general utility to overrun more conformable hues."

Lavin then described her ideal "suburban" house, again showing how thoroughly the Aesthetic Movement fashion for Japanese design had penetrated conventional French décor.

In the sitting room, the surfaces were Japanese, but the furniture was French. The curtains were silk showing blue Japanese figures on a tan ground. There were velour portières, and the doorways were topped by Japanese fretwork. The furniture was Louis XV style upholstered in "old blue."

We shall talk about particular kinds of furniture and objects in the sections on the different styles that made up the Aesthetic Movement. However, all these styles had several themes in common—bringing art into the home, aesthetics as a kind of morality, and a rejection of the middle-class, French prettiness born of the Industrial Revolution.

This 1880 illustration shows an Eastlake-style sideboard, as well as a frieze and beamed ceiling influenced by the Aesthetic Movement.

EASTLAKE OR MODERN GOTHIC: 1875–1880s

Charles Locke Eastlake was the most famous popularizer of the Aesthetic Movement style as purveyed by the South Kensington School in London. The design principles favored by figures such as Christopher Dresser and Owen Jones received wide distribution in Eastlake's popular book, *Hints on Household Taste*. Both in England and America, a large volume of furniture was manufactured following the advice of designers of the South Kensington School, and even at the time, it was called Eastlake. The South Kensington folk themselves would have called it Modern Gothic as they (called Goths) were all propagandists for the Gothic Revival as the only "honest" style.

The other great popularizer of Aesthetic Movement attitudes was Oscar Wilde. As Catherine Frangiamone explains:

In 1882 Oscar Wilde toured America, popularizing the English ideas about decorative design that included admiration for the exotic styles of Japan and the Middle East. In the wake of his visit, Ameri-

can wallpaper manufacturers popularized Moorish motifs, and a style known as "Anglo-Japanese"…. The patterns were rendered commercially in metallic golds, maroon, olive, black, and creamy yellow-beige. Even on the most commercial level during the 1880's a degree of self-conscious interest in "good" flat pattern design and in abstraction was manifested that had never before been apparent and was soon to disappear.

WALLS AND CEILINGS

The Aesthetic Movement wall was different from its predecessors. In the Rococo Revival style of the 1850s and 1860s, walls might be divided into panels by wallpaper moldings, or they might be papered in one pattern from ceiling to baseboard with only small borders at the edges. But the followers of Eastlake and his associates introduced a new sense of proportion. They divided the wall into three parts: the frieze, the field or fill, and the dado.

The frieze was the top part of the wall, usually two to three feet tall with the boldest pattern in the room. It might be a repetitive design of flattened, simplified flowers. Sunflowers and lilies were considered particularly Aesthetic; roses were not. The frieze might be so conventionalized that it became heraldic with fleur-de-lis, anthemions, rosettes, and roses of Lancaster and York. Animals from heraldry and literature were also popular: foxes, chameleons, peacocks, and lions. All of these designs were created in flat color, without shading, in rigidly regular two-dimensional patterns. The bottom edge of the frieze was delineated by a picture molding separating it from the field.

*Top: Eastlake's design for a medieval frieze.
Middle: Aesthetic dado, field, and frieze.
Bottom: Diaper pattern for dadoes.*

The field, which took up the middle of the wall, had the subtlest decoration in the room in order to form a suitable background

Aesthetic Movement three-part wall.

Stenciled dado in diaper pattern.

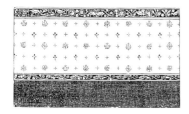

Widely spaced half-step diaper pattern typical of field decoration.

for pictures. It might feature a small figure widely spaced in a diaper pattern. The figure was likely to be symmetrical, two to four inches high, and semi-abstract—for example, an ear of wheat, an Egyptian lotus flower, a fleur-de-lis, a spiky Christopher Dresser abstraction, or a grotesque conventionalized animal.

The bottom of the wall was the dado, three to four feet high with an intermediate scale pattern. It was busier than the field but subtler than the frieze. The top of the dado was the chair rail, now sometimes symbolic and made of paper rather than wood. Because the chair rail was at about the height of a dresser, much of the dado was destined to be hidden by furniture. The dado was usually composed of a continuous web of diaper pattern with each cell four to six inches high.

Eastlake's colors were muddy. Olive was the most popular, with ochre and terra-cotta not far behind. Pink, baby blue, peach, and bright green were never used. There was also a fashion for mixing what we would consider to be clashing colors. A combination we've always liked is the spoiled cantaloupe and salmon pair. Bronze-green and olive were popular together, as were terra-cotta and salmon. Olive with peacock blue was another jarring combination well-liked at the time. Early in the Aesthetic Movement, in the 1870s, there was a feeling that light dull yellow was tasteful and, somehow, Japanese. But that cheerful simplicity did not last long, and the era of yellowy olives was well under way by 1875.

Aside from the new conventionalized patterns and Eastlake colors, an entirely new type of wallpaper was introduced in 1877. Called ingrain paper, it was made by printing the pattern on top of waves of background color shading from light to dark. In this way, it resembled ingrain carpets from which the name was derived.

Aesthetic Movement walls were often decorated with flat, conventionalized motifs in materials other than wallpaper. Lincrusta or Anaglypta could create a different texture for any of the three parts of the wall. Stenciling or bronze powdering was often used for the field, along with a host of fancy paint finishes like glazing, combing, or dragging. For example, varnish could be stenciled on the wall to form a figure, then bronze powder blown onto the varnish to create a shimmering design. Or, coarse sand or gravel would be thrown on the adhesive to create a pattern in contrasting textures. In very grand interiors, the finish coat of plaster might be molded with blocks to create a three-dimensional, repeating, diaper pattern. The sand, gravel, or molded plaster was then painted, varnished, and perhaps bronzed or gilded.

Heraldic stencil pattern for ornamenting the field.

The Aesthetic Movement ceiling also differed from its predecessors. While a cast-plaster ceiling medallion might still be found in most parlors to protect the ceiling from coal gas soot, there were now alternatives. The plaster, central medallion might be replaced with a paper medallion, which did not help with the soot, but satisfied Eastlake's disapproval of three-dimensional ornament on two-dimensional surfaces.

Elaborate interlace pattern suitable for an Eastlake ceiling because it is conventionalized and nondirectional.

The archetypal ceiling decoration was tripartite, much like the wall, with medallion, field, and enrichment taking the place of frieze, field, and dado. Again the field was the subtlest pattern (on the ceiling a nondirectional pattern was usually used) with the enrichment bolder and the medallion bolder still. Just as the three parts of the wall were divided by borders (the picture molding and chair rail), the ceiling parts were also divided by borders three or four inches wide.

There were innumerable variations on this arrangement. The shape of the center portion might not follow the rectangle of the room but, instead, be turned 45 degrees into a diamond shape. Corner ornaments might grow and link up with borders in an elaborate interlace of panels and stripes. The essential characteristic shared by the myriad variations on the three-part ceiling was compartmentalization. The ceiling was almost always divided into sections, and each section is surrounded by substantial bands. In a simplified version of the Aesthetic ceiling, more often seen in bedrooms or simple cottages, the enrichment around the edge of the ceiling was reduced to just a stencil of some spiky pattern like fretwork on a porch or cresting on a roof.

LIGHTING

Eastlake style lighting used the same proportion of gas and kerosene lamps, wall sconces, and gas hose lamps as other styles of the 1870s and 1880s. Generally, gasoliers had straight arms, often square in section. These arms often featured flat ornament of the type popularized by Eastlake and the Aesthetic Movement designer Christopher Dresser. The arms might penetrate a flat brass ring decorated with cut-out Gothic or Eastlake motifs. Often a small crown made of sheet brass decorated the central stem, and struts or brackets of twisted or pierced brass joined the central stem to the arms. The glass shades in Eastlake-style gasoliers were more likely to be straight sided and slightly conical and to display acid-etched designs either Japanese or heraldic in character.

Eastlake-style kerosene lamp.

Kerosene lamps often showed similar design in their cast-brass bases. If the font was ceramic, it often featured an exotic Middle Eastern or Japanese scene. If the font was metal, it generally displayed conventionalized Eastlake ornament. One characteristic of Eastlake-style gasoliers was the fashion for using several metals on one fixture. If red brass, yellow brass, copper, and nickel are used together, the fixture is probably an 1870s or 1880s Aesthetic Movement gasolier, even if it is not very decorated.

Another kind of Eastlake gasolier was made of wrought iron. In exalting the handmade over industrial products, Eastlake favored lighting fixtures made of elaborately twisted and spiral-turned iron rods and bars. These iron light fixtures remained fashionable through the Queen Anne style during the 1880s and 1890s.

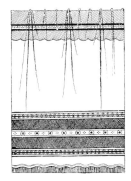

Drapes can follow the frieze, field, dado pattern of the walls in Eastlake rooms.

WINDOWS

Charles Locke Eastlake abhorred heavily draped Victorian windows. In *Hints on Household Taste*, he suggested using substantial rods with big rings supporting simple drapes. Eastlake thought that the pattern and color of the drapes should follow the division of the walls, with a horizontal band at chair rail height and a deep fringe at the height of the baseboard. The end of the curtain rod should have a big finial or spear point to keep the rings from falling off, and that was it—no swags, jabots, *passementerie*, puddling, or ruching. One ornament he recommended was a queen's valance, which consisted of turning the top of a drape forward and attaching the rings at the foldline, creating a short skirt with a fringe.

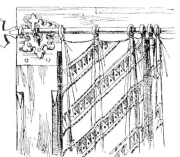

The drapery rod as spear.

Most people who bought Eastlake furniture could not bring themselves to abandon their taste for heavily draped and gathered windows, though exposed rods and simple draperies were seen in very advanced Aesthetic interiors. Eastlake draperies were seldom made of silks, damasks, or other shiny fabrics. Quiet colors and matte finishes

Simple, asymmetrical window treatment with china used as a cornice.

were the norm. Tapestries, velvet, chenille, woolen rep, twill, or kilims created the proper tasteful effect.

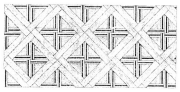

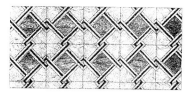

Parquet floors recommended by Eastlake.

Oriental carpet as suggested in Hints on Household Taste.

FLOORS

Aesthetic Movement floors were revolutionarily different from their predecessors. Until the Aesthetic Movement, floors were covered in wall-to-wall carpet. Whether the Aubusson-like roses and cartouches of the Rococo Revival or the anthemions and wreaths of the American Empire, it had been a long time since anyone had seen the wood of a parlor floor. Eastlake's readers learned that their wall-to-wall carpet was unsanitary, tasteless, and positively immoral and followed his advice to rip it up. If the floor underneath was hardwood, like oak, they would varnish it. If the floor turned out to be softwood, like pine, they would paint it, as pine was not considered acceptable looking. Then they would put down individual, oriental carpets, or the new Axminster or Wilton reproductions of oriental designs, or perhaps one of William Morris' new conventionalized foliate designs.

TRIM

Aesthetic Movement millwork was much like Eastlake furniture, with the same repertoire of shapes and decorations. Baseboards were high, as they had been since Greek Revival times, but now sported a band of reeding through the center. The top molding of the baseboard was as likely to be chamfered as to be an ogee, classical molding.

Door casings often had an entirely new arrangement. Instead

of the miter-cornered, classical moldings of the Italianate house, the Aesthetic door-surround usually had base blocks into which the baseboard and the casings butted. The upper corners had head blocks into which the header butted. These head blocks were often ornamented with a zigzag or scalloped crest on the top and incised-line decoration on the front. If there was a wooden chair rail, as in a wainscoted room, the middle of the door casings might feature an additional block to give the chair rail something to butt into. From the mid-1870s through the mid-1880s, the wood of choice was walnut with burl panels ornamenting flat blocks. Black walnut was the choice of wealthy patrons, and pale oak was reserved for the cutting-edge aesthetes. By the 1890s, oak became the predominant middle-class choice, both for furniture and millwork.

Window casings were much like door casings, except that they usually did not have base blocks. Window jambs were sometimes extended to the floor with a fielded panel inserted below to take up the space from the top of the baseboard to the windowsill. Also, various built-in window features became popular during the 1870s and 1880s. For example, window shades, rolling shutters, or interior folding shutters were sometimes included in the window construction.

Axminster rug pattern advocated by Eastlake.

Eastlake incised-line decoration on a newel post.

Reeding, base blocks, and head blocks are the hallmarks of Eastlake-style casings.

FURNITURE AND UPHOLSTERY

According to Eliza Lavin's 1889 advice:

The center table has been banished from its place of honor and the space thus secured is left vacant or occupied by an inviting chair, while near the corners, in window spaces, and wherever there seems to be especial reason for placing them, are little tables of natural wood carved and polished or of less expensive woods finished in imitation of mahogany, cherry, ebony, rosewood, etc. These were draped with scarves or provided with fancy covers, and upon them are placed vases, plaques, statuettes or any ornaments on hand.

Pared-down, Eastlake-style oak bed.

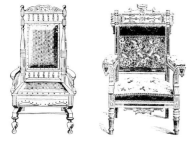

Top: Incised-line decoration and a spiky crest on an Eastlake fainting couch. Bottom: Rectangular backs and seats with crests on chairs.

Most Aesthetic Movement furniture is called Eastlake. Its creators would have called it Modern Gothic, but furniture companies began calling it Eastlake by the mid-1870s despite Charles Eastlake's frequent protests. Most Eastlake furniture is made of walnut with burl walnut panels, unlike the rosewood and mahogany of the Rococo Revival. Eastlake and his fellow South Kensington school designers preferred unvarnished oak, but the commercial versions of their reform furniture were seldom made of oak until the 1890s.

Eastlake parlor chairs and settees were notably less curvy than their predecessors. The chair back was rectangular. The sides of the chair back were formed by reeded stiles. The top of the chair back was a rail with a spiky crest ornamenting its upper edge. The crest and rail were embellished with incised line decoration, panels of burl walnut veneer, and geometric rosettes. The front legs of the chair or settee were usually tapered and reeded, ending in a turned foot supported by a small caster. The upholstery on Eastlake furniture was very different from the Rococo. The aesthetes rejected the clean pastel colors of the Rococo Revival because they were achieved by aniline dyes, an industrial product. Instead, they favored tertiary colors, which they believed more "natural." Edith Wharton grew up in New York in the 1880s and later reminisced that there had been only three colors in her youth, "yellow mud, green mud, and red mud." Those were the Aesthetic colors—ochre instead of yellow, olive instead of green, and terra-cotta instead of red.

Eastlake table.

Eastlake tables generally used some alternative to the traditional formula of four legs, one at each corner. The table top might be marble or wood and usually was a rectangle with its corners clipped off at 45 degrees. Below the table top was an apron with a shield at each corner, corresponding to the clipped corners. The bottom of the apron was usually decorated with a wooden ornament attached at the center of the bottom edge. Eastlake tables were supported in many novel ways. Four legs might extend from the center of the table to a small platform which, in turn, is supported by four splayed legs. Spool-turned columns might join the top and platform, or any version of trusses or flying buttresses could serve as legs.

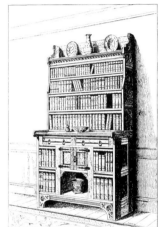

Eastlake bookcase.

Eastlake case furniture featured the same reeded stiles and panels of burl walnut veneer that the chairs and tables had. Incised line decoration was the hallmark of the style, and mirror tops were often bristling with cresting and crockets. Dresser handles, of course, displayed the conventionalized ornament that Eastlake was known for.

Reeding and asymmetrical Japanese ornament decorate an Eastlake armoire.

Aside from the obvious hallmarks of Eastlake furniture—walnut, reeding, incised-line decoration, cresting—its sense of proportion was different from earlier furniture. Where Rococo Revival

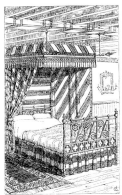

Eastlake recommended this half-canopy hanging from the ceiling.

furniture was substantial, big-bellied, and curvaceous, Eastlake furniture was tall for its width, skinny, and sort of top-heavy. These designers were not trying for elegant and feminine; they were trying for upright and straightforward.

MANTELS

The mantel was often the largest thing in the parlor, as it had been in previous eras. Now, however, the mantel and the overmantel mirror often grew into each other, becoming one monumental construction. In the Rococo Revival, the overmantel mirror was a gilded swirl of plaster of paris moldings. In the Italianate, the mantel was often a semicircular marble arch. In the Aesthetic Movement, the vertical stiles were

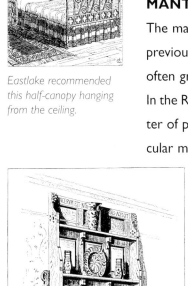

Overmantel as knickknack shelves.

flat walnut with reeding, occasionally interrupted by blocks with burl walnut or incised-line decoration. The top horizontal of the overmantel usually featured a jagged crest of walnut with more incised-line decoration. The mantel shelf was most often rectangular and supported by reeded brackets.

As the Aesthetic Movement wore on and was absorbed into the Queen Anne and Romanesque Revival styles, the overmantel tended to sprout more and more shelves and become an étagère for the display of art objects. They became more and more complicated as the cozy corner, Queen Anne style became more complex as well.

During the 1870s and 1880s, followers of the Aesthetic Movement avoided the matched sets of mantel garniture popular in the 1860s. Instead, they created little still lifes on the mantel with exotic pottery from preindustrial societies such as the Navajo Nation or Arab cultures. Brass from India, pictures, peacock feathers, pampas grass plumes, Japanese fans, and any other bibelots that suggested faraway places or artistic refinement were also displayed. These still lifes were called art units. In their studied informality and their asymmetrical nonchalance, they typify the tenet of the Aesthetic Movement that called for bringing "art" into the house.

PICTURES

Several schools of painting are associated with the Aesthetic Movement. Pre-Raphaelites such as Edward Burne-Jones, John Everett Millais, Dante Gabriel Rosetti, and Lord Leighton are the most famous group, and lithographs of their works were popular in the 1880s. James

Porcelain-headed picture pins.

McNeil Whistler and the Impressionists often used Japanese or exotic elements in their paintings, but few, if any, American homeowners displayed copies of Impressionist paintings until well into the 20th century. High art of any kind, such as chromo-lithographs of Rembrandts and DaVincis, fulfilled the tenet of bringing art into the house.

Photographs, whether of relatives or

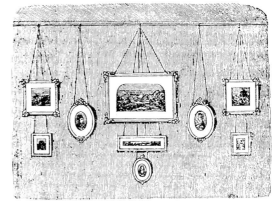

Pictures were hung from long cords held up by picture moldings or picture pins.

of classical statuary, were often placed in narrow, wooden frames featuring incised-line decoration. The mats were often cut into odd shapes or were ornamented with asymmetrical printed-line decoration, pleated fabric, glitter, or glass jewels. Lavin mentions this new emphasis on the picture mats: "The plush frames have been largely superseded by frames of wood burnished or oxidized, with a plush mat or paper mat of velvety effect inside."

Pictures were hung with their cords exposed, usually several at a time, in vertical rows from the picture molding or picture pins (porcelain knobs) placed just under the frieze. By noting an exception to the rule, Lavin demonstrates that the general practice for hanging pictures in the late 19th century was to tilt them out from the wall at an extreme angle. She confirms that, "Contrary to the edict against arranging any picture flat against the wall is the disposal of etchings in small sizes."

EXOTIC REVIVAL: 1880s

When the Aesthetic Movement rejected the Rococo swirls of the French style and the classical vocabulary used in Europe since the Renaissance, they had to look elsewhere for inspiration. They were looking for designs that were two-dimensional to accord with their antiperspective doctrine. And, they were looking for designs from preindustrial societies to confirm their claim that the Western world was going to hell in a handbasket because of the Industrial Revolution. They found what they were looking for in the Middle East.

One of the most popular styles in the Aesthetic Movement was the Exotic Revival. Though few houses were decorated entirely in this style, a nook or corner or smoking room in most middle-class houses would be furnished in Middle Eastern style. During the late 19th century, the Middle East was often in the news. The Ottoman Empire was ever-so-slowly fading after centuries of domination. The English were carving out spheres of influence and were already in control of India. With the new steamships, railroads, and telegraphs, it was not surprising that the imaginations of Americans and Europeans were captured by the Near East as much as by the Far East.

WALLS AND CEILINGS

The walls of an Exotic Revival room were most often divided into the standard three-part Aesthetic division of frieze, field, and dado. If the style was worked into the architecture, spindle-screens or fretwork might be used to create semi-transparent divisions between nooks or bays and the main space of the room. Moveable screens, especially of the carved India-import variety, served the same function. Wallpaper patterns were often derived from the complex Arab interlace patterns found in the Mideast. Because Islamic law forbids the depiction of

Spindle-screen.

human beings as graven images, many Middle Eastern groups developed elaborate foliate and abstract interlaces, often carried out in glazed ceramic tile or mosaic. These arabesques have come in and out of fashion in Europe ever since the crusades, including during the late 19th-century Exotic Revival. These knots and braids were often introduced as a stenciled border around door casings, as well as in the ceiling medallion, frieze, field, and dado.

American and English aesthetes learned about these Islamic patterns from a whole new set of pattern books. *The Grammar of Ornament* by Owen Jones, first published in London in 1856, contained dozens of color plates of Middle Eastern designs neatly divided into ethnic groups such as Moresque and Arabic. Many of these divisions re-

Exotic stenciling surrounding a door.

vealed a sketchy appreciation of Middle Eastern design history, but the book proved immensely popular and was the basis of many wallpaper patterns. Like other Aesthetic Movement figures, Christopher Dresser tried his hand at designing his own Islamic interlaces, often describing them as in "purest" Arab style.

FLOORS

The most radical change wrought by the Exotic Revivalists was in floors. We have already described the switch from wall-to-wall carpet to individual oriental carpets in the Eastlake section of the Aesthetic Movement, but what modern people cannot recapture was the shock value of these oriental carpets. Because we have been putting oriental carpets on the floor ever since the 1880s, they look perfectly natural to us. Imagine being a middle-class homeowner in the late 19th century. The spectacle of individual oriental carpets on a varnished floor, some of them tossed informally on the diagonal, reminded Victorians of the Casbah in Morocco. It called to mind the back alleys of dangerous souks, forbidden harems, European women kidnapped by romantic Bedouins, the underworld of Casablanca, white slavery, and drug traffic. The artistic and bohemian implications of oriental rugs on the floor are lost to us now, but at the time they were a revolutionary rejection of middle-class taste.

A fully upholstered Turkish chair sitting on an oriental carpet in a late 19th-century library.

Egyptian-style chair.

A Turkish easy chair introduced in the 1880s.

FURNITURE

Surprisingly, a lot of Victorian furniture was Exotic Revival, and much of that furniture is still made today. Before the 1870s and 1880s, no furniture had innerspring seats *and* fully upholstered frames. The spiral, innerspring seat that made the "comfy chair" possible was introduced in the 1860s and was first applied to Rococo Revival *fauteuils* and *bergères*. During the 1880s, the club chair and sofa, or divan, were introduced. This new furniture was overstuffed, voluptuous, and sensuous, and all of it was considered Turkish. We still acknowledge the Middle Eastern origin of upholstered furniture in their names. Sofa is an Arab word. Divan is an Arab word. A large footstool is still called an ottoman. During the late 19th century, this furniture still had its Middle Eastern associations and had many of the implications of oriental carpets. After all, this was the first furniture in which it was not necessary to sit up like a lady or a gentleman. It was possible to lounge like a pasha—quite a scandal to a proper Victorian. The upholstery was most often lush and dark—maroon velvet was a favorite. Numerous fringes, tassels, and pillows, with a Middle Eastern tapestry thrown over the back of a sofa completed the decadent scene.

Ottoman.

Another furniture type introduced at this time and considered Middle Eastern was the built-in banquette. Especially for a Turkish corner in a parlor or a smoking room for the gentleman, the built-in banquette was piled with cushions and fringed shawls and covered by an India-import bedspread purchased from Liberty of London. The effect was more 1960s dormitory room than pasha's palace, but the Turkish bazaar effect was an easy one to achieve with a few yards of fabric and some tassels.

TRIM

The door and window casings in the Exotic Revival style were the same as in any Aesthetic Movement interior. However, there were a few embellishments that were peculiar to this version. Horseshoe-shaped, Islamic arches could be easily created in rectangular openings by grouping standard millwork gingerbread in creative ways. Pierced wooden screens that half conceal and half disclose are very characteristic of real Middle Eastern interiors and were often used in Exotic Revival interiors.

Turkish smoking room with Islamic interlace pattern on the walls and ceiling, divan, and Oriental carpets.

The wooden window and door trim of an Exotic Revival room was sometimes outlined on the wall by a band of stenciled, Islamic interlace. The intricate braids and knots of Islamic interlace are particularly suited to stenciling, and late Victorians often executed them in the olives, ochres, and terra-cottas of the day.

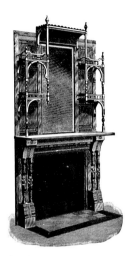

Aesthetic mantel featuring horseshoe-shaped Moorish arches.

LIGHTING

Few built-in gasoliers were designed in Exotic Revival style. Instead, they might be exoticized by hanging a few tassels or shawls from their arms. Lamps, however, were often fashionably foreign. Benares brass vases were commonly fitted out as kerosene lamps. Onion-shaped "mosque lamps" were enormously popular, often with glass jewels inset to glitter in the desert night. More conventional kerosene lamps with ceramic fonts, cast-brass bases, and dome-shaped shades might also be decorated with painted palm trees, pyramids, or silhouettes of camels, all set into a rectangle artfully inserted into an unrelated scene.

WINDOWS AND DRAPERIES

Exotic Revival interiors relied heavily on pinning fabrics up at casual angles, draping them over furniture, and layering them for the Bedouin tent look. As with all the Aesthetic Movement styles, drapes were often hung from rings on a thick brass rod. This was very different from the conventional, middle-class, multi-layered drapery with complicated lambrequins, swags, jabots, and ruchings. The fabrics themselves were seldom

Exotic-berserk wallpaper as well as built-in divans, a Cairene table, screens, and draped furniture.

Middle Eastern, though kilims (flat weave tribal rugs from the Middle East) and tapestries woven in imitation of oriental carpets were sometimes used in this way. Kilims were suitable for portières, bedspreads, sofa throws, drapes, and bed canopies. American- and European-made, multicolored chenille or other fabrics in imitation of tribal weavings, also contributed to the Sheik of Araby effect. Rope portières (nets of drapery roping with tassels) were also used instead of fabric over doorways. In general, it did not matter much whether fabrics were really Middle Eastern, it was the profusion of different, conventionalized patterns draped over every available surface that created the proper effect.

Handmade lamp mat.

Windows were also draped in this way with stripes and patterns layered in artful informality. When possible, Moorish arches were used in pelmets, spindle screens, door openings, and panel designs.

Dresser scarves and tablecloths with pictures of Near East cities, camels, and turbaned natives were woven in the United States. A subgroup was tapestries of Arabs on horseback riding off to the seraglio with kidnapped European women draped across their saddles.

Square table cover for the parlor.

ANGLO-JAPANESE: 1875–1880s

The Anglo-Japanese style was important for about a decade. It was definitely fashionable for aesthetes by 1875 and was pretty tired by 1885. What caused it? Commodore Perry's "opening" of Japan in 1854, forcing the island out of self-imposed isolation, was certainly a precondition. The Centennial Exposition of 1876 in Philadelphia assuredly gave the craze a boost. The style fulfilled the requirements of Aesthetic Movement followers for an inspiration that was the antithesis of the French Rococo. Japan had not experienced an Industrial Revolution. The Japanese did not use Western perspective (that dishonest ploy). And, the Japanese had a rich tradition of "informal" decorative schemes. The English and Americans decided that the Japanese provided a "simpler, more primitive" design source. In reality, the Japanese had an incredibly conventional, exquisitely refined tradition with more rules and restrictions than European classical tradition ever had. It was only with a colonialist's eye looking at the "simple natives" that anyone could have mistaken intensely bureaucratic Japanese society for a more primitive culture.

In its most bohemian, least conventional versions, Anglo-Japanese interiors were uncluttered and light. These interpretations were few and far between, however, and most interiors in this style were just about as decorated and embellished as any other late 19th-century mode.

This Anglo-Japanese room features woodblock prints as a frieze, Japanese fans, screens, and ceramics, as well as little parasols decorating an otherwise Western gasolier.

When modern people think of Japanese design, they think of that part of Japanese culture that the International Style admires—clean, clear spaces divided by moveable rice-paper screens, and rooms without furniture and clutter where one object is isolated like a piece of sculpture. What Victorians saw when they looked at Japanese design was informality and pattern—the repetitive two-dimensional forms in Japanese printed cotton, the layers of patterns on kimonos and obis, the striking graphics of Japanese heraldry, the distorted scenes painted on Japanese ceramics, and the skewed perspective in Japanese paintings.

FURNITURE

A profusion of *japonaiserie* in furniture design developed during the 1870s and 1880s. Some of it was traditional, following the European example of using Asian motifs on Western shapes. Otherwise conventional Victorian sideboards, armoires, or dressers might turn up with bamboo-like turnings to form legs, panels, crests, and cornices. In proportion and type, this furniture was completely European and American. Only the decoration was Japanese.

Both the diagonal fan in this chairback and the wicker material were considered Japanese.

Aesthetic Movement designers also occasionally produced new furniture designs that tried to capture the lightness of Japanese originals. Étagères and tables using square-section, black-lacquered moldings caught the skeletal feeling of Japanese furniture. Small features of Japanese origin, like splayed legs and bold diagonals, also found their way into the design of chairs and occasional tables.

WALLS AND CEILINGS

The three-part wall—frieze, field, and dado—was the most common way of organizing a wall in the Anglo-Japanese style. The wallpaper patterns usually contained explicit and implicit Japanese motifs. Plum blossoms, cranes, swallows, Japanese irises, rising suns, and pagodas all figured prominently in Anglo-Japanese products.

Japanese folding screens with swallows, plum blossoms, and cranes were used to lend an exotic note to Victorian rooms.

Also, more subtle compositional devices were taken from Japa-

Anglo-Japanese designs for door panels.

Anglo-Japanese ornament for a kerosene lampshade.

nese design. Americans saw that objects were cut off by the edge of the picture in Japanese art, that diagonal bands of ornament ran off the picture plane, and that asymmetry was much more common than in the Western tradition. Western designers used these characteristics as cues to make their products look Japanese to their clients. Anglo-Japanese frieze paper might feature diagonal lines of cranes or swallows flying into the distance, plum blossoms, and heraldic disks. The same few motifs were used everywhere—in china, glass, silver, wallpaper, lamps, and book design—to proclaim "Japanese" to the American consumer.

Anglo-Japanese ceilings differed from other Aesthetic Movement styles in their greater tendency to asymmetry. A group of paper fans in one corner of the ceiling, or a flock of swallows flying across it, or different ornaments in opposite corners, gave the ceiling a suitably oriental imbalance.

Japanese materials, such as bamboo or grass matting and grasscloth wallpaper, were sometimes used for wall friezes or ceiling enrichments. Another material employed for wallcoverings was "Japanese leather paper." These textured papers had embossed, three-dimensional medallions and were often painted, varnished, and sometimes gilded. Occasionally these papers were actually imported from Japan but most often were just Japanese style.

FLOORS

The Anglo-Japanese style was seldom so consistent as to extend to the floor. Straw matting was used on floors during the summer in all styles, but Victorians were not consciously being oriental. Middle Eastern rugs were favored in all the Aesthetic Movement styles and were the likeliest choice for Anglo-Japanese interiors. A type of Asian carpet sometimes seen consisted of a large, solid, central rectangle surrounded by a contrasting solid border with flowers ornamenting opposite corners (now curiously called "Chinese Art Déco").

THE WILLIAM MORRIS TRADITION: 1880s–1890s

In the United States, interior design styles and architectural styles were not strictly equivalent during the second half of the 19th century. Early in the 19th century, there had been a clear relationship between American Empire furniture and Greek Revival architecture. Many mid-century Italianate houses had Rococo Revival interiors. But, as the 19th century progressed, the connections grew more and more tenuous. French Second Empire (Mansardic) houses might easily have Aesthetic interiors. Stick Style houses might have Louis XIV interiors. The general conviction remained, however, that particular interior design styles conveyed the same *feeling* as certain architectural styles. This was the relationship between William Morris and the Queen Anne.

Queen Anne-style house.

Queen Anne houses (1885–1900) are the archetypal shape that everyone thinks of as Victorian. While the exteriors sprouted corner towers, turrets, dormers, and bay windows, the interiors were shaped into nooks, crannies, bays, and niches. The Queen Anne was part of the Romantic Movement, the last style in a century-long fascination with romantic medievalism. Instead of reviving the literal motifs of the Middle Ages, as in the Gothic Revival, the Queen Anne style revived the picturesque silhouette, the asymmetrical massing, the lack of classical organization, and the use of many patterns and materials in one house.

William Morris' designs fit in perfectly with the cute cottage, "wee nooke" kind of cozy domesticity found in the Queen Anne house. While his designs are not literally medieval (Gothic), they evoke the vaguely Elizabethan, "olde tyme" feeling that was so loved in this period.

In the Aesthetic Movement there was the split between the conventionalized ornament, Eastlake camp and the natural ornament, Ruskin faction. Though the real relationships among Aesthetic Movement figures were more complex than this division into two camps, William Morris was clearly the most famous member of the Ruskinian group.

William Morris founded Morris & Co., a furniture manufacturer, in London in 1861. He began lecturing on the decorative arts during the 1870s, popularizing Ruskin's view that the decorative arts were not minor but central to creating a moral world. Morris had a house built for himself—Red House—and developed many of the forms and patterns he is known for as furnishings for his own home. His interest in interiors was, oddly enough, primarily moral rather than visual. He was a Socialist and saw design reform as essential for improving the life of the workingman. In accord with the Romantic Movement's dislike of machine-made, mass-produced, overly decorated furniture, he tried to create simple handcrafted furniture for the common man. In the end, none of his company's products were inexpensive enough for working families, nor were his advanced tastes consonant with their preferences. Morris' partners included Dante Gabriel Rosetti, Ford Maddox Ford, Edward Burne-Jones, and Philip Webb.

Morris chair.

FURNITURE

Morris & Co. exhibited its early work at the 1862 Mediaeval Court in London to very mixed reviews. Many critics found the furniture crude and reminiscent of the packing crates in which it was delivered. For the most part, it was simply constructed furniture in box shapes with the sides painted by Burne-Jones and Rosetti as though they were canvases. Soon after the exhibition, the firm turned to lighter, more elegant furniture, mostly designed by Ford Maddox Ford. By 1885, Morris' company was reorganized, and new furniture developed by Philip Webb was produced. This furniture was Gothic, oak, and highly decorated. It was not at all "workingmen's furniture" and allied the firm with more orthodox Gothic Revivalists.

Table with spool-turned legs.

Morris did not succeed in developing a clearly definable style in his furniture. However, there was a definite taste or look to it. Lots of spindles, lightly turned, were characteristic of Morris furniture. The only piece that has remained linked to him is the Morris chair—a reclining chair with spindle sides and separate seat and back cushions—which came in many styles, such as Colonial Revival and Eastlake. Morris did become a successful designer of wallpapers, fabrics, rugs, and accessories. Instead of using a particular furniture style, entire interiors would have a William Morris look by including certain fabric patterns, furniture types, artistic accessories, and art.

Spindle table.

When it came to choosing furniture for these interiors, Morris favored certain styles that were gaining popularity at the time. The early Colonial Revival furniture, where 18th-century authenticity was not the point, was particularly congenial to the William Morris look. Dark varnish on turned legs and stretchers, spindle-screens, barley-

William and Mary style chair with Spanish brush feet.

twist moldings, Spanish brush feet, and squat bun feet—all of these contributed to the cozy cottage look that relied so much on William Morris.

Two furniture styles that gained prominence during this period and were used by William Morris were the William and Mary style and Jacobean Revival. The William and Mary style (confusingly, usually called Jacobean in America) revived the designs of the period from the 1690s to the 1720s. It was characterized by legs formed on a lathe into trumpet-shaped or cup-and-cover turnings. Legs were still joined by turned stretchers with onion-shaped turnings. Chair backs were stiff, tall and paneled, rather than curved with splats. Table tops often sported gadroon edges and were supported by two columns with huge, bulbous turnings, which were in turn supported by H-shaped, cross members.

The second style is the Jacobean Revival which revived the designs of the Stewart Restoration (the 1670s to 1680s). Jacobean Revival furniture was much like William and Mary except that the onion-shaped turnings of stretchers were replaced by flat board stretchers with Baroque outlines and shallow surface carving. Both the Jacobean Revival and William and Mary styles found favor during the period when William Morris' fabrics, wallpapers, rugs, and "olde tyme" picturesqueness were at their height of popularity.

From the first introduction of the Gothic Revival during the 1840s through the end of the 19th century, there was a strong romantic strain that preferred picturesqueness to order, which culminated in the William Morris or Queen Anne look. This preference for variety over organization during the late 19th century is admirably illustrated

Top: Trumpet-shaped legs on a William and Mary style table.
Bottom: Cup-and-cover legs on a 19th-century table.

in a free booklet offered by the Mutual Furniture and Manufacturing Company entitled *Hints on House Furnishing* (1887):

> *It is useless to have a lot of stiff high chairs. Rather vary the seats as much as possible, taking care they are not too high. Convenient ottomans in out of the way angles and recesses are of use, as they relieve the centre of the room.*
>
> *The drawing-room admits of as much freedom of arrangement as you like, under certain graceful restraints. Choose out a convenient spot for your piano-forte, as much in the dark as possible. Then consider the best form of cabinet for your room, and, if possible, place it at the other end away from the piano. A moderate sized writing-table, pedestal, fancy table, or flower-stand may stand in a recess, or window. One or two small tables may also be distributed around the room. A small cabinet for music will generally fit in somewhere along the wall …. Other rooms are more or less of a utilitarian order, but in the Parlor fancy reigns supreme, and our spirits find free scope, unfettered by the weightier cares of life, whatever of poetry, of art, or of culture there is in us, will manifest itself in the furnishing and decoration of the Drawing-room.*

WALLS AND CEILINGS

William Morris wallpapers were, above all, foliate. Sinuous trails of foliage with fruit or flowers created a dense overall pattern. The realism with which Morris' flowers and foliage were drawn contrasted sharply with the severely conventionalized look favored by the Charles Eastlake, Owen Jones, Christopher Dresser crowd. The designs are extraordinarily large to modern eyes and were arranged in an elaborate braid, knot, or interlace of twining stems. William Morris papers often looked like organized cabbage.

The wide frieze found on all Aesthetic Movement walls was common, but the dado was often omitted in the William Morris style. The colors of the wallpapers also varied from the Eastlake branch of the Aesthetic Movement. Whereas the Eastlake fold embraced olives, ochres, and terra-cottas, Morris interiors tended to use somber colors associated with the 1885–1890 period—dark moss green, maroon, and chocolate brown, with accents of gold and vermilion. Morris derived his color schemes from his experiments with natural dyes in reaction to the aniline dyes of the French style of the 1860s.

William Morris paper and fabric design.

WINDOWS AND UPHOLSTERY

In the Queen Anne, American version of Morris interiors, fabrics for draperies and upholstery were often maroon or bottle-green velvet—the materials and colors modern folk often associate with the late 19th century. The idea was to have dark, dull materials in contrast to the shiny ones of the Rococo Revival. Nubby, rough textures like "barkcloth" and burlap were also used as part of the handicrafts, medieval aesthetic. Morris & Co. produced many fabric designs, often experimenting with primitive printing methods, wax-resistant techniques, and vegetable dyes and mordants to recapture the artisanal quality of preindustrial materials. Oddly enough, Morris manufactured light, printed cottons as well. These were often used as café curtains or hung from plain rods to create an informal effect, especially in small cottage interiors or in bedrooms where washable fabrics were considered especially appropriate.

Morris himself designed tapestries for use as wall hangings, draperies, and upholstery. His large allegorical wall hangings were, of course, only suited to the wealthy clients who commissioned them, but middle-class folk did buy medieval-inspired, tapestry-woven cloth for their furniture in imitation of Morris' taste.

FLOORS

William Morris created spectacularly beautiful and complex area rugs. They were designed much like the wallpaper, with organized leaves and flowers arranged in vague approximation of flowing Persian carpets. Commonly named for fabled cities of the Near East, they

William Morris carpet.

did not, however, resemble the typical Bokhara, Heriz, and Isfahans. They were Morris' concoctions combining the complexity of oriental carpets with his own style of foliate ornament. The floors were varnished or painted in Aesthetic Movement style.

RENAISSANCE REVIVAL: 1880S

The Aesthetic Movement style of the 1870s and early 1880s was a reaction against the Industrial Revolution and the ostentation of the new middle class. But what did you do if you were thrilled with the Industrial Revolution and were dying to show off some of your newly earned middle-class money? The answer was the Renaissance Revival of the 1880s.

It is important to note that the Renaissance Revival style was a furniture fashion. Although an interest in the Italian Renaissance began in the mid-19th century, and many public buildings were built in Renaissance style well into the 20th century, we should not exaggerate its importance. Often, earlier styles pervaded all of the details of life. The Greek Revival and the Aesthetic Movement might have affected your hairdo, your dress, your house, your doorknob, your teacup and spoon, even your ethics. The Renaissance Revival style, in contrast, affected furniture and some decorative motifs, but it did not reach into many areas of life.

This headboard shows the massive cornice and scale of the Renaissance Revival style.

FURNITURE

After a decade of meager, incised-line decoration on simple furniture, retailers needed something to appeal to their customers with money. When Eastlake furniture first became fashionable, some people chose it for that reason, not because it was progressive. But it was hard to consider it magnificent or luxurious. So, by the middle of the 1880s, furniture manufacturers grafted big fat cornices onto otherwise

Eastlake furniture. Many of the characteristics of Eastlake remained: incised-line decoration, reeding, burl walnut panels, and tall, narrow proportions. The spiky crest that is so customary at the top of Eastlake furniture disappeared, however, and was replaced by cornices, cartouches, masks of women's faces, keystones, and consoles. No one was bothered by the juxtaposition of Eastlake ornament and classical elements because, by this time, the Eastlake style had lost its reform implications.

Renaissance Revival chair.

The Mutual Furniture and Manufacturing Company booklet, *Hints on House Furnishing* (1887), describes a typical dining room of the day:

> *If the walls of the dining room are dull red, your dining room furniture may be of light oak or very dark. Mahogany or walnut stands well against sage or olive green or dull gray blue. The furniture of a dining room should, of course, be more substantial then that of the drawing-room.*

In addition, the extension table, side table, chairs, and lamps all had to harmonize with each other and with the sideboard.

In the dining room, the effect sought was neither light nor festive, instead, "a certain richness and heaviness of decoration." The "hunt" sideboard with walnut effigies of deer and hares, fish and fruit, became popular. In walnut or black walnut it added a heavy, Teutonic note to mealtimes. This desire for substantial, rich effects in interiors was something new and something Renaissance Revival.

Renaissance Revival sideboard.

There was a new kind of furniture introduced during this period, though not strictly in any style at all—the metal bed. Brass beds and iron beds became very popular with middle-class homeowners, and many bedroom sets offered them as a lighter alternative to the high wooden bedstead. Brass beds were the fancier and iron beds the cheaper version, though both remained popular through the early 20th century independent of style considerations.

A mantel garniture incorporating a bust, sphinxes, and an Ionic capital adds an aura of classical learning to the parlor.

Classical statuary or Victorian versions of classical sculpture became popular decorative objets d'art in the middle of the 19th century and worked their way down the social ladder as cheaper versions became available. While the robber baron or captain of industry might build a wing on his villa to house marbles copied from the antique, as well as bronze and *bronze doré* castings, the middle-class homeowner would display plaster casts or plated, pot-metal statues on pedestals in the parlor. The number of statues that relatively poor people had in their homes would be astonishing to moderns, who generally have no sculpture in their homes at all.

FLOORS

Hints on House Furnishing goes on to recommend Brussels carpet as an inexpensive floor covering, though it acknowledges that "colored India mattings [straw mats] are sometimes used." For the best long-run value, a "Turkey" (oriental) carpet is endorsed. All of these are area rugs. Wall-to-wall carpeting did not reappear until well into the 20th century.

WALLS AND CEILINGS

During the last decades of the 19th century, wealthy Victorians commonly built villas in the country. The art gallery wings of their country manors were filled with the spoils of a "Grand Tour." Both in these country villas and in their city palazzi, these latter-day Medici typically favored marble columns and entablatures as interior decoration. Though this grand Renaissance style was not often imitated by lesser mortals, the fully developed Renaissance interior was a favorite for public buildings and rich men's houses.

Lesser mortals contented themselves with big cornices and paneled walls in their parlors. However, there is no characteristic Renaissance wallpaper. A particularly Renaissance color scheme consisted of tan walls and crimson velvet draperies. Most people probably preferred multilayered drapes, though there was some holdover of Eastlake rod and rings.

A clock and centurion unit combining the virtues of culture and punctuality.

COLONIAL REVIVAL: 1885–1900S

The Colonial Revival is one of the most difficult historical styles to picture because it is still going on. A general awakening of interest in 18th-century design began at the end of the 19th century, and the conviction that pre-Industrial Revolution taste was purer and more elegant has persisted to the present day.

For many, this interest in a lighter, less heavily patterned style expressed itself in yet another "Louis" revival. This is the white-painted, feminine style made famous by Edith Wharton and Ogden Codman, Jr., in *The Decoration of Houses.* For most Americans, though, this nostalgic turning to the 18th century found expression in Queen Anne and Chippendale chairs, rag rugs, and "country" furniture. Looking back at the Colonial Revival through the myriad versions of 1920s, 1930s, and 1940s "colonial" interiors should not distract us from the late 19th and early 20th centuries' Colonial Revival as it really was.

Colonial Revival wallpaper pattern.

During the 1890s, the cozy corner and comfy irregularity of the Queen Anne style was in full swing. The era of spindle screens and Morris chairs was not challenged by the Colonial Revival. At first, the Colonial Revival was not a new look, it was just another set of motifs that had a lot in common with its contemporary Queen Anne.

Much is made of how little the Colonial Revival furniture of the 1880s and 1890s had to do with the furniture of the 18th century. That's because the late Victorians weren't trying to reproduce the 18th century. They were only using it as inspiration for a "creative" revival. Let us picture a Colonial Revival parlor of the 1890s.

WALLS AND CEILINGS

An 1890s Colonial Revival parlor ceiling would most likely be papered with an enrichment, or border and field, just like parlors in the previous 20 years. The walls were generally papered with a wide frieze and fill paper below. The proportions were no different than the Eastlake Aesthetic interior or the William Morris/Queen Anne interior. The frieze was likely to feature American

This Sears wallpaper booklet cover shows the persistence of the Aesthetic frieze, even in stripe and flower Colonial Revival wallpapers.

Empire-style laurel wreaths or swags and drops of delicate bellflower taken from the Adam/Federal design of the period from 1790 to 1830. The area below the frieze was usually papered with alternating stripes and flower sprigs or with vertical stripes of flowers, carrying on the tradition begun with imported French wallpapers of the 1840s. The field might be a widely spaced diaper pattern consisting of laurel wreaths or neoclassical "Adamesque" urns. If the patterns tended toward fluted ovals and swags, contemporaries would have called it colonial or Adam. If it tended toward wreaths, they would have called it Empire. This pertains to a slight variation of the Colonial Revival with vague references to Napoléon's laurel wreaths as emperor of France.

The color scheme for this wallpapered parlor is surprising. Instead of the pale pastels of the 1920s and 1930s Colonial Revival, these papers were usually red and green, red and yellow, or purple and green, as a reaction against the muddy, tertiary colors of the Aesthetic Movement. Clean pastels did not appear until well after the turn

Colonial Revival wallpaper pattern.

of the century. Instead, the trend favored strong primary colors used in complementary contrasts.

A popular alternative to wallpaper schemes for the 1890s Colonial Revival parlor was the use of texture as pattern. Lincrusta-Walton, Anaglypta, and composition moldings had all become popular well before the 1890s. They were made in Anglo-Japanese and Middle Eastern patterns during the 1870s and 1880s. Now they were also available in colonial designs. The shallow plaster decorations of the 1790s were admirably suited to adaptation in the Lincrusta of the 1890s. The wall was again likely to be divided into frieze and fill. The frieze was composed of a deep relief of urns, swags, wreaths, and ribbons. The fill would be a low relief design with more swags and wreaths. The ceiling might be sheathed in Lincrusta featuring the elegant, new, fluted, oval bosses and still more swags. Or, it might be divided into square or elaborate coffers with cast composition moldings.

An "Adam" style Colonial Revival anaglypta pattern.

This Colonial Revival hallway features white painted colonial banister, dado, and bench, as well as huge fern-patterned wallpaper.

These Lincrusta and Anaglypta walls were always painted, then glazed, and sometimes gilded to emphasize their relief. The general effect of these decorating schemes, whether carried out in wallpaper or Lincrusta, was a continuous web of texture and pattern, lightest on the ceiling, boldest in the frieze, and medium for the fill. This continuous web effect is exactly like the other styles of the 1870s, 1880s, and 1890s, and nothing like the colonial interiors of the 1920s and 1930s.

FURNITURE

During the 1890s, people searched their cellars and rummaged through their attics for Grandma's furniture. Often they turned up real Chippendale and Queen Anne chairs, Windsor chairs and benches, and 18th-century "settles." Just as often they unearthed American Empire center tables and console tables from the 1840s, as well as Empire mirrors, chairs, and dressers. All of it got a coat of wax or varnish and went on display as "colonial." It seems extraordinary that people in the 1890s could haul out 1840s furniture and call it colonial. But, if we remember that they meant simpler, preindustrial, and tasteful when they said "colonial," it makes sense. The transformation in interiors was not during the American Revolution but the Industrial Revolution, so everything before the Rococo Revival of the 1850s seemed to go together.

1890s rocker in vaguely colonial style.

No one really furnished their house entirely with 18th-century furniture during the 1890s. The few antiques were there to add a note of class and imply an ancestry with some money. Most of the furniture was modern in Colonial Revival style. The spindle-turning that became so popular in the William Morris/Queen Anne style could just as easily be adapted to the Colonial Revival. In contrast to the bulbous onion-shaped or cup-and-cover turnings and the barley-twist or ball-and-spindle screen transoms, the lathe work became more attenuated. The bulbs became more baluster-shaped, and the Queen Anne doe foot was used for almost everything.

Late Victorians saw no conflict in using 18th-century forms for late 19th-century furniture. Aside from the obvious anachronisms— the colonial electric light, the colonial gramophone, the colonial sewing machine, and the colonial radiator—there were countless, subtle anachronisms created because Victorians were using furniture in ways their ancestors never imagined.

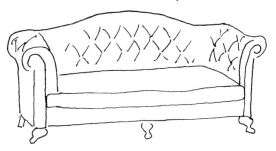

Colonial Revival sofa.

The fully upholstered sofa was an introduction of the 1880s Exotic Revival. By 1900, a camel-back, roll arm version was used in most Colonial Revival living rooms. It was reviving the general form of an 18th-century Chippendale settee, but in a plump, comfy incarnation. Again, the overstuffed easy chair is a "Turkish" Victorian introduction, but with Queen Anne doe feet added, it became colonial. Imagine small 18th-century doe feet straining their delicate ankles to support the mass of a Victorian matron of a chair.

Adamesque mantel with swags and bellflowers.

The arrangement of furniture in the Colonial Revival interior contrasts sharply with the colonial interior. In the Victorian interior, rooms were specialized, and they were crammed with furniture, objects, and patterns. In the Colonial Revival parlor, for instance, a Queen Anne sofa and easy chair might be gathered into a conversational grouping around an oriental carpet with a Windsor chair or rocker or modern deacon's bench rounding out the set. All of these were arranged in front of the fireplace with enough tea tables and lamp tables to allow everyone to read in the evening.

In contrast, during the 18th century, rooms were used for many purposes, and furniture was not plentiful. People did not have sofas and easy chairs, and they did not leave the furniture set up in a conversational group. When the chairs were not being used, they were lined up against the walls. Tables were moved in and out for work and eating, and the only artificial light was likely to be candles, and those were sparingly used. In the evening, people went to bed, they did not sit around the parlor reading.

In the 18th-century colonial dining room, a set of table and chairs, a sideboard, a couple of knife boxes, and perhaps a cellaret comprised all of the furniture. Of course, this describes a wealthy house. Most people set up a table for supper in one of their rooms and moved it away when the meal was over. In the Colonial Revival dining room, the massive table and chairs were supplemented by one or more sideboards, sometimes with a hutch or étagère to display china and silver, and extra lowboys in corners or on piers to hold displays of flowers or large bowls. All of this was topped by an electric, crystal chandelier or a many-armed, brass, Flemish chandelier. Even in a modest, middle-class house, the dining room was used only for dining, and the volume of furniture was staggering.

This Colonial Revival sideboard is really an American Empire shape that has been blown up in size and reinterpreted in oak.

FLOORS

Floors in 18th-century houses were often bare boards scrubbed silver with sand and lye. Painted floor-cloths, druggets resembling heavyweight bedspreads, and straw mats in the summer might have covered the floors. In the Colonial Revival, floors were usually highly varnished oak with elaborate marquetry borders forming Greek keys or other geometric devices. The center of the room was dominated by an oriental design carpet, Middle Eastern in wealthy houses, or European copies like Axminster, Wilton, or even ingrains in less affluent homes.

Druggets were just disappearing as the Colonial Revival style came in. They had been used in dining rooms by many Victorians to keep food from staining the wall-to-wall carpet. The custom of rolling up the carpets and using straw matting for the summer was also fading just as the Colonial Revival style came into fashion.

Victorians associated oriental carpets with colonial interiors. The presence of "Turkey" carpets in colonial inventories and bills of lading was their evidence. In fact, "Turkey" carpets were much too valuable in colonial days to be walked on and were usually displayed on a table or chest as a variety of tapestry.

LIGHTING

By the Colonial Revival, Americans were accustomed to a central, hanging light fixture in parlors and dining rooms. In the parlor, the central ceiling fixture and the center table under it both go out of fashion at the same time, in the first decades of the 20th century. In the dining room, the central ceiling fixture persists to this day, often supplemented by sconces on the walls.

Colonial Revival combination gas and electric sconce.

There were two major types of Colonial Revival "electroliers." By far the most common was the Flemish chandelier—a brass fixture with many S-shaped arms branching out of a central globe or oval-shaped ball. The earliest versions were mixed gas and electric fixtures with the broad, gaslight globes facing up and the narrow, electric globes facing down. When electric service was made more dependable around 1900, all-electric fixtures became common. Sometimes, the bell-shaped glass shades were replaced by porcelain candles with small light bulbs in place of flames. In dining rooms and hallways, matching sconces flanked a central picture above the sideboard.

The second most popular ceiling fixture was the "crystal" chandelier. Derived from the prism-bedecked Rococo Revival gasolier of the 1860s, the Colonial Revival crystal chandelier also featured porcelain candles with small light bulbs in place of flames. Real crystal chandeliers did exist in the 18th century but rarely in America, as they were furnishings fit for noble palaces.

Moveable lighting in the Colonial Revival period bears almost no resemblance to colonial lighting. The Gone with the Wind kerosene lamp with a globular font and matching globular shade finally arrived in the 1890s (it did not exist at the time of the Civil War). Kerosene lamps using Chinese blue-and-white vases as casings for the font with glass or fabric shades were also developed. When electric lamps were introduced, paper or cloth shades were added to the adapted Chinese bases and have continued until today.

Gone with the Wind lamp.

ARTS AND CRAFTS: 1890S–1920S

The Arts and Crafts or Craftsman style was strikingly new in appearance. Not only was the vocabulary of decorative motifs completely unlike what preceded it, but the whole sense of proportion changed. Practically the whole feeling for what was beautiful was different.

In ideas, however, the Arts and Crafts movement came directly out of the Aesthetic Movement. As a reaction to the modern Industrial Revolution, Aesthetic Movement tastemakers romanticized the relationship between a medieval craftsman and his work. Aesthetic Movement books waxed rhapsodic over unvarnished oak with the patina of time. In practice, however, when these designs were translated into mass-produced furniture, that handmade ideal was lost. Especially in America, Eastlake furniture was usually machine-made of walnut and coated with shellac.

The Arts and Crafts movement carried the obsession with the medieval artisan to cult extremes. Setting up utopian communities with the owner as patriarchal feudal ruler, Gustav Stickley and his colleagues continued the Aesthetic Movement's romantic attachment to medievalism. Once again the ideal material was unvarnished oak with wrought iron or beaten copper fittings. But this time, not only the rhetoric but also the furniture was oak. Where the Aesthetic Movement revived the forms of the Middle Ages, the Arts and Crafts movement revived the artisan system and material of medieval furniture.

WALLS AND CEILINGS

The walls of a Craftsman-style house were organized in a new way. The dado grew until it met the frieze and squeezed out the field entirely. Imagine a bungalow's parlor. The walls were horizontally divided by an oak rail about six feet above the floor. The area below the rail was likely to be separated into tall, narrow panels by flat, oak battens. These panels might be filled by painted plaster or painted burlap, canvas, or grass-cloth. Above the rail, the wall could be painted the color

of the ceiling or papered with a frieze of silhouetted shade trees. One wall was dominated by a bulky fireplace built of exposed red brick, iron-spot brick, or Roman brick, with a corbeled mantel shelf above. The ceiling of the parlor was either coffered or beamed with paneled oak or plaster painted to look like oak. The general effect was as though everything had been made into panels with dark oak dividing walls and ceiling into grids.

The colors of the Arts and Crafts movement were also new. Where the Aesthetic Movement had preferred olive, terra-cotta, and ochre, the Arts and Crafts

An Arts and Crafts parlor with an exposed-brick fireplace. The walls and ceilings are divided into rectangles by oak trim.

preferred moss green, maroon, and oatmeal. The palette was still somber, especially with all that dark oak trim. The colors were no longer tertiary but were primary and secondary colors of dark value and medium intensity. The other great difference was that the Arts and Crafts movement always preferred a matte finish. The Aesthetic Movement had a great fondness for bronze powderings on walls, gilt in wallpaper and furniture, and irregular glazes in pottery. In the Arts and Crafts, the shine was entirely gone. Oatmeal paper was popular when wallpaper was used. Burlap and canvas provided rough textural interest to set off the dark stained oak. Even in pottery, where shine is hard to avoid in glazes, Roycroft and Rockwood pots pioneered a new matte finish.

Arts and Crafts parlor.

Another contrast between the Arts and Crafts and preceding styles was the rejection of pattern. In the Aesthetic Movement every surface in the room was part of a continuous web of two-dimensional pattern. The interplay of fine and coarse pattern in complex wallpapers and upholstery was a large part of the style. In the Arts and Crafts, all of that was gone. Most of the time, there was no pattern. Flat painted walls and the texture of wood, burlap, oatmeal paper, and woolens replaced pattern altogether. Of course, there were exceptions. The frieze might easily include silhouetted trees or a rectilinear pattern. In addition, the top third of each wall panel might feature a geometric ornament. The drapes or curtains might feature a woven-in Navajo or other tribal design instead of being plain wool. The floor might display a Navajo rug or a flat, woven kilim from the Near East. However, even if all these exceptions were present, it still would be largely a room of flat color with incidents of pattern, a far cry from the 1880s room made entirely of interlocking patterns with hardly a break.

TRIM

The oak trim was generally wide and flat, rejecting as anathema the curved moldings of the classical tradition and the elaborately reeded and chamfered look of the Aesthetic Movement. Window and door trim also avoided the mitered corners characteristic of Italianate interiors and, instead, opted for post and lintel, pilaster and entablature format.

LIGHTING

During the early 20th century, electricity finally became dependable enough to entirely supplant gas. Ceiling fixtures in Arts and Crafts style were of two main types. A living room without a center table would frequently have no ceiling fixture at all. If there was a center table, the light was likely to be a chandelier made of square section, brass tube with downward facing, square section, glass lamp shades shaped like bells. Whether there was a central ceiling fixture or not, sconces (of similar design to the chandelier) probably flanked the fireplace and might punctuate the other walls.

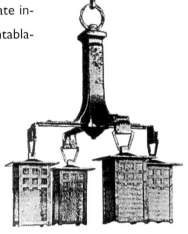

Arts and Crafts chandelier.

Arts and Crafts sconce.

The other kind of ceiling fixture, almost always shining down onto a dining table, was a large, dome-shaped lamp made of oak or copper or brass with amber colored, opalescent glass panels. This dining room lamp might be constructed like a stained-glass lamp or made of wood framing with glass panels.

Table lamps in this style almost always had a pedestal base and a dome-shaped shade. The base would be an oak box with sloped sides or a cast-brass or bronze treatment. The shade might be an oak-framed box with opalescent glass panels, a shallow glass dome reverse-painted with silhouettes of trees, or a shallow stained glass dome with Art Nouveau leanings.

Arts and Crafts table lamp.

Craftsman linen and canvas curtains.

WINDOWS

A thick brass or wooden rod with brass or wooden rings supporting heavy, dark, woolen drapes was the classic Arts and Crafts arrangement. In a high-style house, the rod and rings might be square instead of round.

Variations on this theme included replacing wool with canvas, coarse linen, or net. Materials to be avoided were silks and satins, printed chintzes, jacquards, damasks, or any floral or shiny fabric.

FURNITURE

Trestle table with ostentatious pegged joinery.

Arts and Crafts furniture was as rectilinear as the rooms. Glorying in the "honesty" of its design, Arts and Crafts furniture was largely comprised of square section oak posts and slats, joined together with ostentatiously prominent mortise and tenon and pegged joinery. The religious avoidance of curves in molding or outline led to some of the most uncomfortable chairs and sofas ever made. But the consistent use of flat slats and square legs in boxy compositions did create some monastically beautiful furniture. In fact, Arts and Crafts designers did succeed in reviving the discomfort that the packing-crate furniture of the Middle Ages must have caused its owners.

The arrangement of furniture in the Arts and Crafts parlor was also new. To start with, the parlor was now just as likely to be called a living room. The nook and cranny irregularity of the Queen Anne interior was gone. The myriad "fairy tables" and unmatched Morris chairs and easy chairs were gone. Even the center table, standby of every 19th-century style, was gone.

Arts and Crafts armchair.

Instead, the rigidly rectangular ruled. Not only in the divisions of the walls and the design of the furniture, but also in the placement of the furniture—everything was at right angles. The

Stickly settee.

settle was perpendicular to or facing the fireplace. The coffee table or tea table was aligned. The sideboard, the easy chairs, and everything else is either lined up against the walls or around a rectangular rug laid straight in front of the fireplace. At most, one massive easy chair might be moved ostentatiously to 45 degrees to suggest an "informal" seating arrangement—a far cry from the Aesthetic Movement's diagonal Casbah style of arranging oriental rugs and parlor chairs on wheels.

UPHOLSTERY

Arts and Crafts furniture also had its characteristic upholstery. Where the Rococo preferred damask, the Aesthetic preferred conventional flat patterns, the Queen Anne sought out William Morris patterns, the Arts and Crafts opted for brown leather. The upholstery was most often confined to boxy, innerspring slip-seats, as the fully upholstered, Turkish easy chair or sofa was far too comfy and decadent for the monastic image of the Arts and Crafts.

Craftsman studios rug.

Brown leather was the preferred upholstery.

DOMESTIC OFFICES

Victorian houses included more than the public rooms and bedchambers. They also contained the service spaces—the practical, the necessary, the working rooms of the house. During the 19th century, these were often called the domestic offices.

BATHROOMS

In 1889, Eliza M. Lavin wrote, "No dwelling is complete without a bath-room, and the preceding illustrations prove that even a small cottage may be provided with one without curtailing the dimensions of other rooms."

In the illustrations, there is a large tub and small foot bath, but no toilet. Lavin literally meant bath-room.

Bathroom facilities such as sinks with running water, bathtubs, and toilets, were introduced individually and became common at different periods. The first bathtubs were tin-plated metal and had to be filled with pots of water. They were placed in front of the fireplace, usually in bedrooms, and removed when not in use. As early as the 18th century, there is occasional mention of a bath-room in France and England, though not in America.

Running water was introduced into houses as a pump in the kitchen. By the 1840s, a boiler as part of the stove apparatus was not unheard of, and pipes could supply hot water to the kitchen or perhaps a ground-floor room. A cistern in the attic, refilled by rainwater or well water pumped up, could supply running water to an upstairs faucet by mid-century. But people still washed at washstands with a pitcher and a bowl for 40 years longer. The first city-supplied running water was in Philadelphia in the early 19th century, followed by New

Washstands were standard equipment in Victorian bedrooms.

York City with the building of the Croton Reservoir system in 1846. A distributing reservoir at 42nd Street and Fifth Avenue in New York supplied piped water under pressure throughout the city, but this kind of service did not reach small towns until the 1890s.

Americans used outhouses well into the 20th century. The water closet was available by the 1880s, but many people were skeptical about how sanitary it would be to have one in the house. People in larger cities and towns started using indoor toilets first, as digging another hole in the backyard for the outhouse was not always easy. For a long time, however, indoor hot and cold running water was much more common than water closets. Also, until the water trap and vent

Washbowls and pitchers persisted even after bathrooms were introduced.

was developed, the problems of "sewer gas" or methane bubbling up the drain from the cesspool threatened. Sewer gas was smelly, poisonous, and explosive. After years of failed experiments with techniques to control sewer gas, homeowners were understandably reluctant to expose their families to disease, poisoning, and possible incineration. The inventor who developed an efficient flush toilet was, indeed, the eponymous Thomas Crapper.

So, all the parts of a bathroom came together during the 1880s. Early bathroom fixtures were largely sheathed in wood with beadboard wainscoting

A high-style Eastlake bathroom from the 1880s, complete with high-tank toilet and foot bath.

and wooden cases for tub and toilet. Beadboard was the normal wall covering for all sorts of utilitarian spaces: store rooms, kitchens, outhouses, and bathrooms. It might be painted or grained and varnished.

The "Victorian" bathroom that we think of—matte white hexagonal floor tiles, white tile dado with a decorative top, claw-foot tub, pedestal sink—is an improvement of the 1890s and really did not become standard until after 1900. Freestanding fixtures and exposed pipes were a sanitary feature that was considered

The white tile "sanitary" bathroom style of the turn of the century still has the same basic facilities.

an improvement over the earlier built-in schemes. The white, washable surfaces and visible pipes enabled homeowners to avoid the dark, damp, vermin-infested corners that had plagued earlier versions of the indoor bathroom.

KITCHENS

Kitchens, like bathrooms, evolved with new technologies rather than the changing fashions of interior decoration. During the 18th century, a modest house usually did not have a kitchen. The hall and parlor house plan consisted of two multipurpose rooms: the hall for cooking, eating, and chores; and the parlor for paperwork, needlework, reading, and, sometimes, sleeping. Cooking was done in the fireplace with the help of a myriad of jacks, pots, tin ovens, and blacksmith's implements. This was the way people had cooked from time immemorial.

Cast-iron stove.

In more affluent houses, kitchens were in separate buildings, or sometimes in basements, to avoid the smell and the danger of catching fire. Especially in city houses, the basement or an "L" in the backyard was the most likely site for the kitchen. In the early 19th century, cast-iron stoves that burned wood were introduced and immediately became popular. Kitchens still remained in a separate building, especially in the South where the heat was not welcome.

By the middle of the 19th century, kitchens often had a number of built-in features. In *The American Woman's Home, or Principles of Domestic Science* (1869), Catherine Beecher and Harriet Beecher Stowe recommended a counter with built-in bins below to hold large quantities of staples such as flour, beans, and potatoes. Built-in cabinets with shelves concealed by doors were not uncommon to hold dishes and crockery. A sink with pump or faucet, depending upon the availability of city water, was attached to one wall. It was usually made of cast iron with a drainboard attached or standing adjacent. Open shelves holding groceries and hooks for implements lined the walls, while a table and chairs for cooking and eating dominated the middle of the room.

Food storage on legs was considered a sanitary measure, as in this "refrigerator," as ice-boxes were called.

Beadboard was the preferred wall covering, sometimes for the dado, sometimes for the whole wall. The floor was likely to be bare wood scrubbed with lye and sand. Sometimes an oilcloth or floor cloth went under the table. From the mid-century onward, a new industrial product made of linen canvas and linseed oil was used as a floor covering. It was named linoleum, combining the words linseed and oil (oleum).

An efficient Victorian kitchen with built-in bins in the mid-19th century.

Toward the end of the 19th century, a new sanitary style for kitchen design was introduced. Instead of built-in bins and cupboards, there was a move to freestanding storage on legs. Sink supply pipes

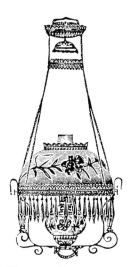

This type of kerosene lamp was used in kitchens, although the prisms shown here are too fancy.

Meat grinders and cherry pitters were among the dozens of gadgets introduced in the late 19th century.

and drain lines were left exposed. As much as possible, everything was raised on legs so floors and walls could be scrubbed. This improved air circulation and allowed rodents and insects to be spotted. The new linoleum was even used as a scrubbable wainscoting, though painted beadboard remained much more popular.

Lighting in kitchens was always rudimentary. From the mid-century onward, kerosene lamps and gas fixtures were used. The gas fixtures were completely undecorated pipes descending from the ceiling with either one plain gas burner or T-shaped with two burners. The lamps might be unshaded or have the simplest, cheapest shades available. Kerosene lamps were suspended in a cast-iron or brass harp. When electricity was introduced, the bare bulbs hung from the ceiling by their wires.

In the late 19th century, the contents of the kitchen changed dramatically. John Henry Kellogg introduced prepackaged cereal during the 1880s and was soon followed by Charles W. Post with Postum and Post Toasties. The National Biscuit Company invented sanitary packaging by wrapping crackers in waxed paper and a cardboard box. While Gail Borden canned his new "evaporated milk," everyone else canned vegetable soups and meats. Late 19th-century kitchens were filled with boxes and cans of prepackaged brand-name foods, instead of large quantities of unprocessed "natural" staples stored in barrels, sacks, and jars.

Another major difference between the early and late 19th century is the introduction of many laborsaving devices. The early 19th-century kitchen was equipped with pots and pans, knives and forks, bowls and platters. The late 19th century saw the introduction of egg beaters, ice shavers, washing machines, can openers, pressure cookers, apple peelers, cherry pitters, meat grinders, and a thousand other gadgets to make kitchen work easier through technology.

CLOSETS

For much of the 19th century, the word "closet" didn't mean built-in clothes cupboard. It referred to any small room. In the book *Jane Eyre,* Jane says she sleeps in a closet. In England the little room with the plumbing is still delicately referred to as the W.C. or water closet, and some older people still specify the closet used for clothing storage as a "clothes closet."

Victorian clothes closet.

The question remains, why do Victorian houses have so few clothes closets? The popular answer is that they were considered rooms, and houses were taxed based on the number of rooms. This is not true. Victorians stored their clothes in trunks and boxes and hung up only the current outfits in the armoire. As long as labor was cheap, as it was after the Irish potato famine of the 1840s, there was no incentive to make clothes storage more convenient. The lady of the house wrote down her choice for the next day's outfit on a card and left it on her dresser. Maids fetched the clothes from a box room upstairs, pressed them, and laid them out. Only with the restrictive immigration quotas of the 1920s do closets expand and multiply in American houses.

Victorian storage trunk.

There are exceptions to this rule. The George Allen house (1863) in Cape May, New Jersey, for example, has huge walk-in closets for each bedroom. The architect, Samuel Sloane, was a pioneer in believing that convenience—storage, central heat, ventilation, and daylight—was important in domestic architecture. Almost no one followed his lead, however, for another 50 years.

DECORATIVE ELEMENTS

C reating authentic Victorian rooms does not just depend on the right furniture and wallpaper. It is as much a product of the proper ornamental objects and ephemera as of the appropriate large appointments. Many of the bibelots in 19th century houses transcend style and express other values in Victorian life.

SEASONALITY

In furnishing a Victorian room, modern folk should keep in mind how different summer and winter were during the 19th century. In the spring much of the household furniture was cleaned. This meant bringing the carpets outside and beating them with wire or cane beaters to remove the dust. The upholstered furniture was similarly whipped and aired. The rugs were then rolled up and stored in the attic in paper or cloth sleeves to protect them from moths and sun-fading. The chairs were slipcovered in plain cotton or ticking stripes. The floors were either bare or covered with inexpensive straw matting. The drapes were also removed and, if needed, were washed or spot cleaned with kerosene or naphtha. Then they were folded, wrapped, and put away for the summer. Gasoliers and gilded picture frames were washed and enclosed in cheesecloth bags to keep off flys and flyspecks. The whole house was washed down to remove the winter's soot from the woodwork, walls, and ceiling. Gauze curtains were hung across the bottom half of many windows as bug bars, and mosquito nets were often hung around the beds, especially in the South, giving the whole house an almost tropical look.

All of this work was reversed just after Labor Day in preparation for the coming season. The summer mattings and slipcovers were stored in the attic. The potted palms were returned to the parlor from the garden and porch. The antimacassars reappeared on the upholstery, and the family got ready for Thanksgiving and Christmas.

PLANTS

From the middle of the 19th century onward, the Victorians developed a strong interest in decorating with houseplants. The boom in houseplant culture reflects several Victorian developments. The Industrial Revolution made the discovery and importation of exotic, tropical plants possible and introduced central heating that allowed tropical plants to survive the winter in the north. Also, the Victorian Romantic Movement made bringing nature into the home an admirable activity.

Plant stand from the 1880s.

Wealthy households that could afford a conservatory often incorporated one into the house. Less affluent people set aside a bay window or at least a Wardian case (named for its inventor). It was discovered that if exotic plants were put in a glass box, watered and sealed, the plants would survive a long sea voyage without needing any maintenance. Soon thereafter, many Victorians made terrariums or Wardian cases in their libraries and filled them with miniature landscapes of ferns and bracken. The most popular Victorian houseplants could survive on little light. Clivia, aspidistra, Spathiphyllum, and the India rubber plant were popular for the heavily curtained and shaded interior. Potted palms in the parlor are legendary, of course, and were often displayed in globular, Benares brass containers on pedestals. Most Victorian furniture styles had fern stands and plant stands aplenty picturesquely placed in parlors, on landings, and in halls. Strikingly colored or patterned leaves were always welcome, making coleus, a recent introduction from South Africa, a popular garden and houseplant.

TAXIDERMY

One of the most peculiar Victorian tastes was the widespread use of stuffed animals, heads, horns, and hooves as decorative items. Even odder to present-day thinking is the fact that the fondness for animal parts in the parlor was part of the same feeling that produced the conservation movement. By the middle of the 19th century, the burgeoning growth of cities as a result of the Industrial Revolution lent a note of nostalgia to country life. The frontier was closed and the transcontinental railroad built by the late 19th century. People felt that all of the wild places would soon be tamed. This impetus eventually led to Teddy Roosevelt's establishment of the national parks. It also led to the fashion for African safaris and big game hunting. Victorians venerated nature, but they never imagined that animal species could become extinct. Though the passenger pigeon and the bison were on their way out even at the moment, Americans saw no harm in having a stuffed memento of the wilderness to ornament the parlor. Elephant feet as umbrella stands, hooves or horns as inkwells, stuffed birds under glass domes, tiger-skin rugs and throws, Indian mongoose and cobras frozen in mid-battle, furniture made of cattle horns, and mounted heads all found their way into the well-furnished Victorian home.

A cow's head made a tasteful ornament for the library.

An interesting sidelight to the fascination with taxidermy is that it was considered a good hobby for the genteel Victorian lady. Advertisements in Victorian newspapers offered stuff-at-home lessons for women who desired a delicate activity for their leisure hours.

COLLECTIONS

The assembling and display of collections was a direct expression of the mid-19th-century Industrial Revolution. Victorian homes held three kinds of collections: art, nature, and exotic souvenirs. Collections of art objects were part of the Aesthetic Movement. They came out of the feeling that the Industrial Revolution had debased modern taste and that an artful home could serve as an antidote to the philistine world. Collections of natural objects—rocks and minerals, shells, leaves, and fossils—were part of the general feeling that scientific and technological progress were daily improving the world. Middle-class people wanted to be part of the worldwide spreading of knowledge. Exotic souvenirs were evidence that the collector was widely traveled or at least was familiar with faraway places. Steamships and railroads brought distant continents within reach of newspaper reporters and wealthy travelers. Ordinary people heard about developments in the Ottoman Empire, South Africa, and Japan.

An extraordinary collection of "primitive" exotic objects.

DOILIES

Victorians seemed to live in fear of naked furniture. Perhaps that's why they invented so many kinds of furniture underwear—lacy, filmy, delicate, and feminine covers for bare tabletops, pianos, mantels, and dressers. In general, no horizontal surface was left uncovered. Doilies, dainties, scarves, and antimacassars were vehicles for the lady of the house to display her crocheting, cross-stitch, crewel, Berlin work, tatting, drawn thread, ruching, and lace. These examples of the needle woman's art expressed the exaltation of handwork over machine-made. They also contributed to the idea, born out of the Aesthetic Movement, of the home as a temple of art.

Each style had its favorite cloth covers: flowery lace in the Rococo; Japanese-style, cherry blossom embroidered scarves in the Anglo-Japanese; Turkish tapestries in the Exotic Revival; and coarse linens in the Arts and Crafts. Almost everyone draped the mantel with a lambrequin, the chair backs and arms with antimacassars, and the bookshelves with dust skirts. Where a cloth wouldn't fit—for example, on a picture frame, a lampshade, or an easel—a premade bow called a tidy bow would provide that perfect accent.

BEDSPREADS

It is sometimes difficult to know what bedspreads are appropriate for period bedrooms in various 19th-century styles. Many kinds of bed-spreads existed and remained available from their introduction through the rest of the century, often to the present.

A crazy quilt adds a Japanese note.

The American Empire era saw the introduction of several new kinds of loom-woven bedcoverings, as well as the continuation of several 18th-century, handmade types. Trapunto, or whitework coverlets, were created by quilting elaborate designs onto a white ground. Also during the American Empire era, many motifs such as large wreaths or medallions were used in trapunto. The background was quilted in a fine cross-hatching of diagonal lines. There was an-other, similar, class of bedcoverings where the base fabric was coarse linen instead of fine cotton and the background of the pattern is worked in parallel lines instead of cross-hatching. This was called Sicilian cable work and really was a product of small, southern-Italian communities in America during the early 19th century.

Both patchwork and appliqué quilts and throws are appropriate bedcoverings for the entire 19th century. Small patterns and solid colors in elaborate, geometric designs characterized the entire period, though there were a few style differences. Crazy quilts and throws where there is no organized pattern were considered Japanese-looking because of their picturesque asymmetry. These were used in Aesthetic Movement bedrooms more than other styles. Quilts that featured fan motifs were also considered Japanese and were associated with the 1870s and 1880s. Of course, the muddy, Aesthetic Movement colors found their way into quilt-making and help date them. Aesthetic Movement needlework was also expressed in elaborate, decorative topstitching on crazy quilts of the 1870s and 1880s.

The overshot coverlet, in which some of the threads over-shoot the weft to create the design, were produced by small-scale weavers who often traveled around the country. They were popular from the beginning of the 19th century through the 1850s and were made in hundreds of designs. Most commonly in indigo blue and white, they are appropriate for American Empire and simple Rococo Revival bedrooms.

Overshot coverlet

Jacquard coverlets were made on a loom invented in the 18th century by Joseph Jacquard. They were introduced into America in the 1820s and remained popular through the 1860s. Complex pictorial designs were possible using prepunched cards to guide the loom. The Jacquard cards are a favorite illustration of the origins of computer programming, but they are important for period interiors because they made complicated bedcovers available to middle-class homeowners at a moderate cost.

Jacquard coverlet.

Candlewicking spreads, which resemble modern chenille bed-spreads, were popular throughout the 19th century. Originally, they were made by embroidering unshrunk cotton cloth with thick cot-

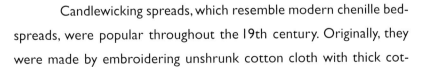

ton thread left in loops on the right side of the fabric. The spread was then washed. The shrinking captured the embroidery threads and then the loops were cut, creating a fringed line pattern. These were introduced in the 1820s and were mechanized in the 1840s. They remained through the Colonial Revival era, at which time they were revived as a colonial bedcovering.

An interesting handcrafted bedcover that would be easy to recreate is the stenciled coverlet. Stencils, similar to those used for other purposes, were used on cloth bedspreads. The dyes were blended with oil or gum arabic and the resulting patterns washed to set the dye. These bedcovers were made at home throughout the 19th century.

Marseilles or Marcella was another bedcover material popular through the Victorian era. It was a heavy, white, corded material with a pattern woven in. It resembled whitework and chenille and is still available today. Matelasse was a waffle-woven fabric often used for bedspreads. It also resembled whitework quilting and was an inexpensive machine-made alternative.

With a large graining roller, no skill was required to create woodgrain effects.

FANCY PAINT FINISHES

The use of commercially prepared, standardized paints came with the Industrial Revolution. Because painters no longer had to grind their own white lead and mix it with linseed oil, turpentine, and pigments on site, fashions in paint could be disseminated more quickly. During the second half of the 19th century, fancy paint finishes such as graining, glazing, and stippling were part of every professional's repertoire. Paint companies had an interest in changing fashions in colors, and they succeeded admirably.

Nineteenth-century wall paint was usually oil paint. Distemper, or water paint, was not washable and was confined to utilitarian spaces like kitchens that would otherwise have been whitewashed. Calcimine paints were washable but only came in pale colors that were generally used for kitchens and sometimes ceilings. A Victorian painter would prepare a wall for oil painting by sizing it. If the homeowner was prudent, the painter would line the walls with linen to prevent cracking. Several coats of oil paint were then applied in opposite directions to minimize brush marks created by the "ropy" paint. In the final coat, extra turpentine would be added to cut the shine, and the surface would be stippled with a large brush that looks like a scrub brush to create a non-directional, matte finish.

Many subtle patterns were created in paintwork by varying the final coat. If the final coat were semi-transparent and in a different color than the base, the resulting glaze could be dragged (subtle parallel lines created by a dry brush), combed (strong parallel lines created by steel or rubber combs), rag-rolled (an overall pattern created by a rolling cloth), or sponged (an overall pattern created with a sponge).

On top of the painted finish, an overall diaper pattern was often created by stenciling. The stenciled decoration might be done by stippling a contrasting color of paint. Or, gum arabic could be stenciled in a design and then bronze powder blown onto the adhesive. Alternatively, the pattern could be stenciled in adhesive and have sand or even gravel thrown at it. Sometimes real or patent gilt was applied to a stenciled design. All of these techniques were used for any part of the wall—dado, field, or frieze. But subtle patterns and contrasts were most associated with the field, while bolder patterns and contrasts were used in the dado and frieze. Stencils with several

Top: Stenciling brush and stenciled dado.
Bottom: Graining rollers for quick graining in 1879.

parts forming the shape, shadows, and highlights of a three-dimensional trompe l'oeil design were strongly associated with non-Aesthetic interiors. Wall panels were often created this way in Rococo Revival interiors. Late 19th-century Queen Anne or Colonial Revival interiors used this technique to create classical cornices.

The woodwork in most Victorian styles was varnished, but there were notable exceptions. All of the French styles allowed for off-white trim, often glazed and wiped off to emphasize the moldings. In grand houses, parts of the trim might also be picked out in gilt.

Graining was common throughout the 19th century. Greek Revival doors were grained to look like mahogany. Rococo Revival doors were grained to look like rosewood. Aesthetic Movement woodwork was grained to look like oak. Despite the Aesthetic Movement's condemnation of graining as dishonest and tasteless, people continued to rely on it as an inexpensive alternative to costly hardwoods. Many kitchens were grained to look like oak. Amazingly, the kitchen woodwork at Lyndhurst in Tarrytown, New York, is made of straight-grained oak grained to look like quartered oak.

Marbleizing was a widely held skill during Victorian times, but it was used with discrimination. During the 1880s, slate mantels or even wood mantels were often marbleized to look like black marble with gold veins. Cast-iron architectural elements molded in the shape of stone, such as columns, pilasters, or modillions, were often painted in imitation of marble. But the architectural element would only be marbleized if it could plausibly have been made of marble. The Aesthetic Movement, of course, condemned marbleizing as a sham, but the condemnation seems to have had little effect. Eastlake style mantels were marbleized just as often as any other, perhaps even more.

Dragging brush for creating subtle lines or pores in graining.

Stippling brush for an overall pattern.

Leather comb for creating woodgrain or combed finishes.

GREEK REVIVAL / AMERICAN EMPIRE: 1835–1850s

In this American Empire scene, notice the period carpet—a large-patterned, ingrain carpet installed wall-to-wall. The door surround reveals that this is a Greek Revival room, and the window swag and jabots are in the same style. The secretary-bookcase in the next room shows how simple American Empire furniture was and how heavily it relied on figured veneer and interesting silhouette for its effect. Although the small tables and rocking chair are not American Empire, they are correct for the time. Plain, painted walls are also appropriate for this era and are very different from what follows later in the century.

FRENCH STYLE / ROCOCO REVIVAL: 1850s–1860s

The Belter chairs in the center of the parlor represent the most extreme version of the Rococo Revival: the carving has so overwhelmed the chair frame that the roses and S-curves have become the frame itself. The marble-topped center table continues the curve of the chairs, as does the more modest side chair next to the mantel. The fireplace, which is more Italianate in style, is topped by a Rococo Revival gilded mirror. The wallpaper, which resembles copper-plate engravings, has just the right character, scale, and color for this period room, but the subject of the engravings is Gothic, as this is a Gothic house. The rug is a little old-fashioned in taste to go with the chairs but is just the kind of intense color that mid-century burghers liked. The draperies are very simple for this kind of room, but the elaborate gasolier is a perfect companion for the Rococo chairs and table.

FRENCH STYLE / ROCOCO REVIVAL: 1850s–1860s

This drawing room displays almost all of the features that a luxe Rococo Revival room could have. The walls are divided in panels by Rococo moldings. The furniture is encrusted with foliate carving. The mantel is a white marble patisserie of leaves, fruit, and flowers. The rug is a perfect rose-colored, rose-scattered Aubusson design. The mirrors are immense French plate glass with gilt frames. The gasolier is a two-tiered bronze doré extravaganza. The only thing missing from the room is cloth. The windows, no doubt, had acres of pastel silk damask cascading from the cornices and puddling on the floor. The tables and mantel probably had handmade lace covers and doilies under bowls of bourbon roses.

HIGH VICTORIAN GOTHIC:
1860s–1870s

Few cathedrals could compete with this elaborate Gothic dining room. The woodwork is arched and cusped, the chairs resemble stained glass windows, and the carpet is diaper patterned. Even the windows (glimpsed in the mirror) look ecclesiastical. In this room the walls are Gothic, the fireplace is Gothic, the light fixtures are Gothic, probably the food was Gothic.

HIGH VICTORIAN GOTHIC: 1860s–1870s

This headboard could be the door of a church. The label lintels above the door and casement window show that the room's architecture is Gothic. The cusped cabinetry of the bed and dresser are Gothic as well.

THE AESTHETIC MOVEMENT:
1875–1880s
EASTLAKE

The extreme simplicity of this mantel, designed by Frank Furness in 1879, with its large scale, reeded brackets and geometric, turned rings, represents cutting edge Aesthetic Movement design. The tertiary colors of the ceramic tile and the heraldic-looking spades on the mantel face also accord with Furness's Aesthetic tastes. At the time, the varnished oak floor with oriental carpets was also radically artistic. The French-style molded frieze and ceiling decoration are not part of the original scheme and date from an 1890s redecoration.

THE AESTHETIC MOVEMENT: 1875–1880s *EASTLAKE*

None of the ornament that most of his contemporaries thought essential appears in this bed designed by architect Frank Furness. Instead, Furness used hard-edged, mechanical-looking motifs and plain surfaces. The bedcovers are hand worked whitework, and the wallpaper is a William Morris design in a light color scheme suitable for bedrooms.

Top left: Christopher Dresser, an English Aesthetic Movement leader, developed this design for powderings. The colors are muddy: olive for green, terra cotta for red, and ochre for yellow. The motif is flat and conventionalized as Aesthetic Movement dogma dictated. Designs like this were intended to be used widely spaced in a diaper pattern on the field of a three-part wall. They would have been applied as a stencil with paint or bronze powder.

Top right: The ceiling medallion pattern in "Arab" style was also designed by Christopher Dresser. He suggested it as a stencil, though it seems hopelessly complex. Flat paper medallions accorded with the Eastlake/Dresser dictum that three dimensional ornament should not be used on flat surfaces.

Bottom left: This stenciled Gothic dormer ceiling shows how complex the craft could be.

Bottom right: This tile fireplace surround shows the color scheme most favored by Aesthetic designers in the 1870s and 1880s.

This spool-turned, lathe work furniture would have been called Elizabethan in the 19th century. Many such so-called historical styles contributed to the quaint, old-fashioned, cottage-like appearance that was so popular for the last third of the 19th century. Introduced in the mid-century, this kind of bed was used as a middle-class alternative to high style Rococo, Italianate, and Gothic bedsteads. It became more popular as the century went on, until it went out of fashion at the turn of the century and came to be called the "hired man's bed."

RENAISSANCE REVIVAL: 1880s

The walls of this late Victorian Renaissance Revival bedroom are papered in a French-style pattern resembling toile de Jouy fabric. Oriental carpets on the floor reveal that this room was furnished after the Aesthetic Movement had had its effect. The grand furniture features large cornices, keystones, and extensive paneling. Its pale color, in contrast to the dark wood of most Renaissance Revival beds, indicates that it was probably designed for a woman's bedroom. The French style chair reinforces that impression.

The cottage furniture in this bedroom illustrates a design tradition that continued through the second half of the 19th century. Cottage or painted furniture was a light and inexpensive alternative to the substantial Italianate and Rococo style of the public rooms. It was used by poorer people or for secondary spaces and was available in Italianate, Rococo, Anglo-Japanese, Eastlake, Exotic, and Colonial Revival styles. Trompe l'oeil panels and painted burl and marquetry enlivened otherwise simple case pieces, while flowers were either hand painted or added by decals.

EXOTIC REVIVAL: 1880s

This house is higher style than an ordinary Exotic Revival interior because it was custom-built for the painter, Frederick Church, in a style he called "personal Persian." Beginning with the arched openings and the Islamic interlace stenciled walls, continuing onto the Turkish carpet-strewn floors, and including the fireplaces, furniture, and myriad objects, this room is the epitome of exoticism. Notice the heavily draped and fringed tables, the kilim used as a portière, the brasses and ceramics. Everything contributes to the late Victorian setting of a pasha's palace.

ANGLO-JAPANESE:
1875–1880s

This Anglo-Japanese parlor shows many of the features of the style: Anglo-Japanese paintings, bamboo, and the ubiquitous paper parasol. The frieze paper includes cherry blossoms, diagonal lines, and Japanese heraldic disks. The field is combed and stenciled to resemble bamboo. An angular Eastlake cast-metal gasolier lights the room. Eastlake style chairs, tables, piano, and an oriental rug complete the 1880s Aesthetic interior.

COLONIAL REVIVAL: 1885–1900s

This very late 19th-century parlor has many elements that are Colonial Revival, several that are French, and a few that are Exotic. The Colonial Revival elements include the door surround with its swag and drop motifs and oval, fluted bosses taken from the Adam Brothers. The mantel repeats similar swags, and the ceiling includes swags forming a continuous S-curve, though this might have been considered French at the time. In the foreground, a Chippendale chair, table, and the upholstered chair near the fireplace were also Colonial. If this were a more thoroughly Colonial Revival room, it would probaby have a flower and striped wallpaper instead of the French style damask wallpaper, the sconces and candlesticks would be more Georgian and less Louis, and the lincrusta pattern of the frieze would be more swag and urn and less Rococo.

ARTS AND CRAFTS: 1890s–1920s

This thoroughly Arts and Crafts grouping includes high-style furniture, lamp, and pottery from the early 20th century. The matte finished oak in its distinctive dark craftsman color, the brown leather upholstery, and the dull gleam of the period pots contrast with the shine and shimmer of earlier Victorian styles. Were this a bungalow or other Arts and Crafts style house, the walls would have been divided into vertical panels by broad flat oak trim, and the surface of the panels would have been sheathed in burlap, canvas, rough plaster, or oatmeal paper.

This bathroom illustrates the beginnings of the new sanitary style of the late 19th century. The sink's pipes and legs are exposed rather than installed in furniture-like cabinets. This enabled the floor to be scrubbed all the way to the base-board and left no place for vermin to hide. The floor is wood, however, and the walls are painted. By the turn of the century, both would have been tile.

BIBLIOGRAPHY

Banham, Joanna, Sally MacDonald, and Julia Porter. *Victorian Interior Design*. New York: Crescent Books, 1991.

Burke, Doreen Bolger, et al. *In Pursuit of Beauty: Americans and the Aesthetic Movement*. New York: The Metropolitan Museum of Art; New York: Rizzoli International Publications, 1986.

Calder, Jenni. *Women and Marriage in Victorian Fiction*. New York: Oxford University Press, 1976.

Davidson, Marshall B., and Elizabeth Stillinger. *The American Wing at the Metropolitan Museum of Art*. New York: The Metropolitan Museum of Art and Alfred A. Knopf, 1985.

Downing, Andrew Jackson. *Cottage Residences; / or, / A Series of Designs / for / Rural Cottages and Cottage Villas, / and their / Gardens and Grounds. / Adapted to / North America*. 1873. Rpt. as Victorian Cottage Residences. New York: Dover Publications, 1981.

Dresser, Christopher. *The Art of Decorative Design*. 1862. Watkins Glen: The American Life Foundation & Study Institute, 1977.

Dresser, Christopher. *Studies in Design*. 1876. Rpt. as The Language of Ornament: Style in the Decorative Arts. New York: Portland House, 1988.

Dubrow, Eileen, and Richard Dubrow. *Furniture Made in America 1875-1905*. West Chester: Schiffer Publishing, 1982.

Eastlake, Charles L. *Hints on Household Taste in Furniture, Upholstery and Other Details*. 1878. Rpt. as Hints on Household Taste: The Classic Handbook of Victorian Interior Decoration. New York: Dover Publications, 1986.

Fitch, James Marston. *American Building 1: The Historical Forces that Shaped It*. 2nd ed. New York: Schocken Books, 1973.

Frangiamore, Catherine Lynn. *Wallpapers in Historic Preservation*. Washington, D.C.: U.S. Department of Interior, 1977.

Gist, Noel P. and Sylvia Fleis Fava. *Urban Society*. 5th ed. New York: Thomas Y. Crowell Company, 1964.

Jacobs, Bertram. *Axminster Carpets*. London: F. Lewis, 1970.

Jarry, Madeleine. *The Carpets of Aubusson*. London: F. Lewis, 1969.

Kasson, John F. *Rudeness & Civility: Manners in 19th-Century Urban America*. New York: Farrar Straus and Giroux, 1990.

Lavin, Eliza M. *Home-Making and House Keeping*. New York: Butterick Publishing Company, 1889.

Lynn, Catherine. *Wallpaper in America*. The Barra Foundation, 1980.

Maril, Nadja. *American Lighting 1840–1940*. West Chester: Schiffer Publishing, 1989.

Mayhew, Edgar deN., and Minor Myers, Jr. *A Documentary History of American Interiors: From the Colonial Era to 1915*. New York: Charles Scribner's Sons, 1980.

McGee, Harold. *On Food and Cooking: The Science and Lore of the Kitchen*. New York: Charles Scribner's Sons, 1984.

Meyers, Denys Peter. *Gaslighting in America: A Guide for Historic Preservation*. Washington, D.C.: U.S. Department of Interior, 1978.

Moss, Roger W. *Lighting for Historic Buildings: A Guide to Selecting Reproductions*. Washington, D.C.: The Preservation Press, 1988.

Mutual Furniture and Manufacturing Co. *Hints on House Furnishing*. Mutual Furniture and Manufacturing Co., 1887.

Nylander, Jane C. *Fabrics for Historic Buildings: A Guide to Selecting Reproduction Fabrics*. 4th ed. Washington, D.C.: The Preservation Press, 1990.

Pierson, William H., Jr. *American Buildings and Their Architects: The Colonial and Neoclassical Styles*. Garden City: Anchor Books, 1976.

Pine Press Editors. *Lamps and Other Lighting Devices, 1850–1906*. American Historical Cata-logue Collection. Princeton: The Pine Press, 1972.

Poulson, Christine. *William Morris*. Secausus: Chartwell Books, 1989.

Safford, Carleton L., and Robert Bishop. *America's Quilts and Coverlets*. New York: Weathervane Books, 1974.

Saisselin, Remy G. *Bricabracomania: The Bourgeois and the Bibelot*. London: Thames and Hudson, 1985.

Schlereth, Thomas J. *Victorian America: Transformations in Everyday Life, 1876–1915*. The Everyday Life in America Ser. New York: HarperCollins Publishers, 1991.

Schlesinger, Arthur Meier. *The Rise of the City, 1878–1898*. A History of American Life Ser. 10. 1933. Chicago: Quadrangle Books, 1971.

Seale, William. *The Tasteful Interlude: American Interiors Through the Camera's Eye, 1860–1917*. 2nd ed. Nashville: American Association for State and Local History.

Victoria and Albert Museum. *Wallpapers: A History and Illustrated Catalogue of the Collections of the Victoria and Albert Museum*. London: Sotheby Publications, Victoria and Albert Museum, 1982.

Wharton, Edith and Ogden Codman, Jr. *The Decoration of Houses*. 1902. New York: W. W. Norton & Company, 1978.

Winkler, Gail Caskey, and Roger W. Moss. *Victorian Interior Decoration: American Interiors 1830–1900*. New York: Henry Holt and Company, 1986.

GLOSSARY

Acanthus leaf In classical architecture, a decorative leaf modeled after the deeply cut leaf of the plant *Acanthus molis*.

Anthemion A stylized honeysuckle flower used as decoration in classical architecture.

Antimacassars Cloths used on chair backs to keep hair oil from staining the upholstery.

Appliqué "Applied" in French, meaning a glued-on surface ornament.

Arabesques A curved, twining design in decorative arts, named from its use in Arab ceramics and architecture.

Architrave In classical architecture, the bottom part of an entablature. Also sometimes used to describe a window or door-surround.

Arrises A sharp edge made by two surfaces meeting, as in the edges of the flutes on a fluted column.

Aubusson A French carpet manufacturer. By extension, a French-style carpet featuring large roses.

Baluster A vase-shaped vertical support for a horizontal hand rail.

Balustrade A row of balusters topped by a horizontal rail.

Barley-twist moldings Spiral turned elements often used as legs on "Elizabethan" style furniture.

Battered Leaning in at the top. A battered door-surround or wall is narrower at the top than the bottom.

Bead and reel An enrichment of a classical molding representing a string of beads in which disks alternate, singly or in pairs, with oblong beads or "olives."

Beadboard wainscoting A wooden wall covering consisting of narrow boards and half-round moldings, arranged vertically.

Bergère A wide French easy chair of 18th-century design with exposed wooden frame and upholstered seat, back, and arms.

Batten A narrow, vertical strip of wood.

Boss A disk covering the intersection of two ceiling ribs.

Bronze doré "Gilded bronze" in French.

Buttress In Gothic architecture, an extra support for a wall, either part of the wall or extending from it.

Cabriole legs Curved furniture legs consisting of a broader knee tapering to a narrow ankle, characteristic of French, Queen Anne, and Chippendale furniture.

Carcass The box of case furniture, as distinct from its drawers.

Cartouche In architecture or furniture, a panel or shield, often resembling leather, often carrying heraldic devices or a monogram.

Castellated Having battlements like a castle.

Cavetto In classical architecture, a cove or hollow molding.

Chamfered Having the 90-degree edge of a square molding modified with a narrow 45-degree band.

Coffer In classical architecture, a recessed ceiling panel, usually square or octagonal.

Colonettes Small or thin columns.

Composition moldings Furniture moldings made of sawdust and glue or a similar material.

Console In classical architecture, a vertically oriented scroll-shaped bracket, as opposed to a modillion which is horizontal.

Corbel A bracket made of bricks in which each course projects beyond the course below.

Cornice The crowning member of a wall, or part of a wall. It is the top part of a classical entablature.

Cove molding A hollow molding creating a shadow, called cavetto or scotia in classical architecture.

Cresting An ornamental member, or a group or series of members, used to form a decorative finish at the top of any structure, as along the ridge of a roof. A continuous feature.

Crocket In Gothic architecture, a decorative feature carved in various leaf shapes and projecting at regular intervals from the angles of spires, pinnacles, canopies, and gables.

Cupola A small decorative structure on the roof of a house, usually an Italianate, low-pitched roof.

Cusped In Gothic architecture, something which has sharp points.

Cyma recta An S-curved molding with the beginning and ending of the S in an horizontal position.

Dado The bottom part of a wall in a three-part wall division, or the base of a statue.

Diaper A repetitive pattern whose alternate rows are set off a half-step, forming diamond shapes.

Doe foot A furniture foot found on cabriole legs in Queen Anne furniture, resembling the foot of a deer.

Doric One of the classical orders of architecture with columns that are taller and slimmer than Tuscan, but less slim and ornamented than all the other orders.

Druggets Inexpensive floor cloths often used on top of more expensive carpets to catch food under a dining room table.

Egg and dart An enrichment of a classical ovolo molding which resembles alternating eggs and darts.

Entablature In classical architecture, the horizontal element supported by columns. The entablature consists of the architrave, the frieze, and the cornice.

Étagère A "shelf unit" in French.

Fairy tables Small lightweight tables.

Fan vaulting In Gothic architecture, ceiling vaults in which ribs radiate like a fan.

Fasces The ancient Roman emblem of civil authority: a number of rods bound together with an ax into a cylindrical bundle.

Fauteuil A light French armchair of 18th-century design with exposed frame and upholstered seat and back.

Fillet In classical architecture, a small flat molding.

Finial A boss, a knob, or a more elaborate ornament at the point of a spire or pinnacle.

Foliate Leafy.

Fretwork Interlaced openwork such as a meander or a Greek key.

Frieze In classical architecture, the middle portion of an entablature. In wallpaper, the top part of a three-part wall division.

Gadroon In silver or furniture, an edge treatment consisting of a row of angled bumps.

Gesso A material which can be molded into decorations, or the sizing used by artists on canvas.

Glass-curtains Sheer curtains that are closest to the glass in a window treatment.

Greek key A repeating fret.

Ingrain or scotch carpet A narrow loom, woven carpet with a reversible design introduced in the 1840s.

Ionic One of the classical orders of architecture, most memorable for the volutes of its column capitals.

Jamb The vertical side member of a door or window frame.

Lintel A beam or the like over an opening which carries the weight of the wall above it.

Loggia An Italian word for a porch set into the mass of a building.

Lowboy A short chest on legs, as opposed to a tall chest on legs which is called a highboy.

Mantel garniture A set of decorative objects for furnishing a mantel shelf.

Medallion A generally disk-shaped tablet, panel, or similar member, treated decoratively or forming part of a decorative composition of which it is the central or a prominent feature.

Miter A bevel or oblique cut on each one of two parts which are to be joined end to end at an angle.

Modillion brackets In classical architecture, a bracket with S-shaped sides that supports the cornice.

Mortise and tenon A joint in woodworking consisting of a hole in one member and a tongue that fits into it from the other member.

Mosque lamps A brass lamp resembling an onion, popular in Exotic interiors.

Muntin The wooden member that separates the panes of glass in a window.

Newel post The post at the base or head of a flight of stairs.

Objets d'art "Art objects" in French.

Ogee An S-shaped molding.

Ovolo An egg-shaped molding like a quarter-round.

Illustration Credits

Palazzi "Palaces" in Italian. These are usually city houses as opposed to villas, which are country houses.

Passementerie Trim on upholstery and drapery, like braid, fringe, or tassels.

Pediment The low triangular gable following the roof slopes over the front and rear of a classical building.

Pelmet A flat cloth panel at the top of a window in a window treatment.

Pilaster In classical architecture, an engaged pier with a flat face, projecting slightly from a wall surface, and furnished with a capital, base, etc., as if to correspond with a column.

Portière Drapes used in a doorway.

Post and lintel Also called post and beam. Two verticals supporting a horizontal.

Puddling In drapery, allowing fabric to drag on the floor for a luxurious effect.

Quatrefoil In Gothic architecture, a four lobed motif.

Rep A ribbed cloth made of wool or silk.

Roller-blind A window shade.

Ruching Plaited, quilled, or goffered strips of lace used as an edging.

Rusticated In ashlar masonry, a treatment emphasizing the joints.

Spanish brush feet Furniture feet used on William and Mary furniture, resembling brushes.

Splayed Spreading apart at the bottom.

Stiles The verticals in a paneled door or furniture, as opposed to the rails which are horizontal.

Strapwork In Elizabethan or German Baroque architecture, decoration resembling leather straps.

Stretcher The horizontal member which joins the legs of a chair.

Swag and jabot A window treatment consisting of a gathered horizontal cloth at the top of the window flanked by pleated triangles.

Trefoil In Gothic architecture, a three-lobed motif.

Trompe l'oeil "Fool the eye" in French.

Tuscan order One of the classical orders of architecture. The plainest and squattest one used for utilitarian settings.

Valance A short skirt used as a window top decoration or a mantel cover.

Volute A spiral scroll, as in an Ionic capital

Wainscot The lower part of a wall, especially when sheathed in beadboard.

Waterleaf molding An enrichment of a classical cyma recta molding resembling a repeating leaf.

Photographs © 1995 by Tim Fields pages:
17: Old Merchant's House, New York, NY; 18: Ebenezer Maxwell Mansion, Philadelphia, PA; 21 (bottom): Taylor-Grady House, Athens, GA; 22 (bottom): Old Merchant's House, New York, NY; 43: Ebenezer Maxwell Mansion, Philadelphia, PA; 50 (top): Wilderstein Preservation, Rhinebeck, NY; 51 (bottom): Victoria Mansion, Portland, ME; 52: Acorn Hall House Museum, Morristown, NJ; 55: Park-McCullough House, North Bennington, VT; 57 (top): The Delameter House, Rhinebeck, NY; 62: Lyndhurst, A Property of the National Trust for Historic Preservation, Tarrytown, NY; 63 (bottom): Henry Bowen House, Roseland Cottage, Woodstock, CT; 76 (top): The Emlen Physick Estate, Cape May, NJ; 81 (bottom): Olana State Historic Site, New York State Office of Parks, Recreation, and Historic Preservation, Taconic Region, Hudson, NY; 82 (top): Acorn Hall House Museum, Morristown, NJ; 83 (bottom): Victoria Mansion, Portland, ME; 96: Park-McCullough House, North Bennington, VT; 97 (bottom): The Abbey Bed & Breakfast, Cape May, NJ; 98: Colvmns by the Sea, Cape May, NJ; 119 (top): The Emlen Physick Estate, Cape May, NJ; 123: Lyndhurst, A Property of the National Trust for Historic Preservation, Tarrytown, NY; 124: The Emlen Physick Estate, Cape May, NJ; 129: Old Merchant's House, New York, NY; 130: Ebenezer Maxwell Mansion, Philadelphia, PA; 131: Victoria Mansion, Portland, ME; 132 and 133: Lyndhurst, A Property of the National Trust for Historic Preservation, Tarrytown, NY; 134 and 135: The Emlen Physick Estate, Cape May, NJ; 136 (bottom left): Lyndhurst, A Property of the National Trust for Historic Preservation, Tarrytown, NY; 136 (bottom right): The Emlen Physick Estate, Cape May, NJ; 137: Acorn Hall House Museum, Morristown, NJ; 138: Park-McCullough House, North Bennington, VT; 139: Acorn Hall House Museum, Morristown, NJ; 140: Olana State Historic Site, New York State Office of Parks, Recreation, and Historic Preservation, Taconic Region, Hudson, NY; 141: Leith Hall Historic Seashore Inn, Cape May, NJ; 142: Wilderstein Preservation, Rhinebeck, NY; 143: The Queen Victoria, Cape May, NJ; 144: Lyndhurst, A Property of the National Trust for Historic Preservation, Tarrytown, NY.

Drawings © 1995 by Elan Zingman-Leith pages: 16 (top), 21 (top), 22 (top), 24 (top, middle), 25 (top, bottom), 27, 31 (top), 34, 35 (bottom), 45 (top), 46 (bottom), 47 (top), 54 (top, bottom), 61 (middle), 82 (middle), 89, 90, 91 (bottom), 97 (top), 104 (top), and 107.

Additional sources pages: 65: *American Architect and Building News.* New York, March, 1878; 66: Leith Hall Historic Seashore Inn, Cape May, NJ; 68: *American Architect and Building News.* New York, March, 1878; 69 (middle), 70 (middle, bottom) and 71 (top, bottom): *A Decorator, the Paper Hanger, Painter, Grainer and Decorator's Assistant.* London: Kent & Co. Publishers, 1879; 73 (bottom): *American Architect and Building News.* New York, 1887; 75 (middle, bottom): Sash, Doors, Blinds, Mouldings catalogue; 79 (bottom): *A Decorator, the Paper Hanger, Painter, Grainer and Decorator's Assistant.* London: Kent & Co. Publishers, 1879; 85 (top): *Ladies Home Journal*, December 1887; 85 (bottom): *Ladies Home Journal*, December 1885; 86: *Artistic Houses: Being a Series of Interior Views of a Number of Beautiful and Celebrated Homes in the United States.* 4 vols. New York: Appleton, 1883-1884; 88 (top): Sash, Doors, Blinds, Mouldings catalogue; 88 (bottom): Pittsburgh lamps 1885; 94 and 95: Morris, William. *William Morris Full-color Patterns and Designs.* New York: Dover Publications, Inc., 1988; 99: Adams Quincy Franklin clocks 1885; 100: *A Decorator, the Paper Hanger, Painter, Grainer and Decorator's Assistant.* London: Kent & Co. Publishers, 1879; 104 (bottom): A.S. Nichols manufacturers of mantels, grates, tiles … catalogue; 110: Brooks catalogue 1908; 115 (bottom): *American Architect and Building News.* New York, 1887; 116 (top): *The Decorator and Furnisher,* June 1891; 117 (bottom): Beecher, Catherine Ward and Harriet Beecher Stowe. *The American Woman's Home,* 1869; 126, 127 (top, bottom) and 128 (top, middle, bottom): *A Decorator, the Paper Hanger, Painter, Grainer and Decorator's Assistant.* London: Kent & Co. Publishers, 1879; 136 (left, top right): Dresser, Christopher. *Authentic Victorian Decoration and Ornamentation.* New York: Dover Publications, Inc., 1986.

Private collection pages: 23 (top, bottom), 24 (bottom), 26, 35 (top), 36 (top), 41: Thomas Nast, Nursery tales "There He Is"; 42 (top, bottom), 44, 45 (bottom), 46 (top), 47 (bottom), 48, 49 (top, bottom left, bottom right), 51 (top), 53 (top, middle), 60 (top), 61 (top), 70 (top): William Willer Sole Manufacturers of Willer's Sliding Blinds; 72, 76 (bottom), 77 (top, bottom), 82 (bottom), 83 (top), 84 (top), 87 (top, bottom), 91 (top, middle), 92 (top, bottom), 103, 105, 106, 114, 115 (top), 116 (bottom), 118 (top, middle, bottom), 119 (bottom), 121, 122, 125 (top, bottom).

INDEX

William Morris, 95
oilcloth, 117
painted floor-cloths, 23, 105, 117
Renaissance Revival, 98
Rococo Revival, 36-37, 47
staining floorboards, 59
Ford, Ford Maddox, 90, 91
France
carpetmaking in, 36
French plate glass, 40-41
French wallpapers, 17, 18, 20, 37, 39, 47, 50, 55, 59
Frangiamore, Catherine, 17, 19, 37, 39, 58, 68-69
French Second Empire (Mansardic) houses, 89
French Style (1880s-1890s), 48-49, 131
furniture, 49-50
lighting, 51
walls and ceilings, 50
French Style/Rococo Revival (1850s-1860s). *See* Rococo Revival (1850s-1860s)
frieze and field
Aesthetic Movement, 69-70
Anglo-Japanese style, 87-88
Arts and Crafts style, 108-9, 110
Colonial Revival, 101
Eastlake design, 69-70
Furness, Frank, 134, 135
furniture
Aesthetic Movement, 49, 75-78, 82-83, 87, 91-93
American Empire, 14-17
Anglo-Japanese style, 87
Arts and Crafts, 112-13
bentwood, 35
Colonial Revival, 103-5
cottage, 139
Eastlake-style, 75-78, 96-97
Exotic Revival, 82-83
French-style, 49-50
Gothic Revival, 57-58
Hepplewhite, 14
Italianate, 52-53
Jacobean Revival, 92
Japanese, 87
Louis XVI, 48, 49
Marie Antoinette, 48, 49-50
William Morris, 91-93
oak, 48
Renaisssance Revival, 53, 96-97
Rococo Revival, 33-35, 52-53
William and Mary style, 91, 92

gas burners, 24, 42
gas fixtures, in kitchens, 118
gas sconces, 47
gas table lamps, 44
gaslighting developments, 51
gasoliers
Aesthetic Movement, 72-73, 84
cast-iron, 43
Eastlake-style, 72-73

Exotic Revival-style, 84
Gothic, 60
Greek Revival, 26
Rococo Revival, 43
gasoline, 42
George Allen House, Cape May, New Jersey, 119
glossary, 148-50
Gothic architecture, Aesthetic Movement and, 65
Gothic Revival (1845-1850s), 56-57
floors, 59
furniture, 57-58
lighting, 60
walls and ceilings, 58-59
windows, 60-61
See also High Victorian Gothic (1860s-1870s)
graining, 128
graining rollers, 126, 127
The Grammar of Ornament (Jones), 81
Greek Revival/American Empire (1835-1850s), 14-16, 129
bedcoverings, 124
bedroom, 28-29
floors, 23
furniture, 16-17
lighting, 23-26
pictures, 27-28
trim, 21-22
walls and ceilings, 17-20
windows, 26-27

High Victorian Gothic (1860s-1870s), 57, 132-33
walls and ceilings, 62-63
Hints on House Furnishing (MFMC), 93, 97, 98
Hints on Household Taste (Eastlake), 68, 73
Home-Making and House Keeping (Lavin), 66-68, 75-76, 79, 80, 114
houseplant culture, 121
Hyde Park, New York, 9

ice-boxes, 117
illusionistic wallpapers, 18-19
Impressionist paintings, 79
India rubber plants, 121
Industrial Revolution, 8
Aesthetic Movement reaction to the, 64, 80, 123
American Empire and the, 20
Arts and Crafts movement and the, 108
discovery of exotic plants during, 121
Renaissance Revival and the, 96
Italianate (1860s)
floors, 55
furniture, 52-53
mantels, 35-36, 54-55
walls and ceilings, 53-54
windows, 55

jabots and swags, 26, 27, 45
Jackson, Andrew, 14

Jacobean Revival furniture, 92
Jacquard coverlets, 125
Jacquard, Joseph, 125
Jane Eyre (Brontë), 119
Japan
Aesthetic Movement fashion for Japanese design, 67-68
See also Anglo-Japanese (1875-1880s)
Jennings, Isaiah, 25
Jones, Owen, 68, 81, 93

Kellogg, John Henry, 118
kerosene lamps
Anglo-Japanese kerosene lampshade, 88
Eastlake-style, 72-73
Exotic-Revival-style, 84
Gone with the Wind, 51, 107
Gothic, 60
invention of kerosene, 42-43
in kitchens, 118
Rococo Revival, 42-43, 47
kilims, 85
kitchens, 116-19

laborsaving devices, 118-19
lambrequins, 60-61, 124
lamps
agitable oil, 24
Arts and Crafts style table, 111
astral oil, 25
banquet, 51
burning fluid, 25-26, 43
camphene, 25, 43
gas burners, 24, 42
gas table, 44
gaslighting developments, 51
Gone with the Wind, 51, 107
Harvard lamp, 43
lamp mat, 85
lard burning, 25
mosque, 84
oil, 24-25, 44, 47, 60
sineumbra, 25
solar, 25
student lamp, 43
whale-oil, 24
See also chandeliers; gasoliers; kerosene lamps
Lavin, Eliza M., 66-68, 75-76, 79, 80, 114
Leighton, Baron Frederick, 79
lighting
Arts and Crafts style, 111
Colonial Revival, 106-7
Eastlake-style, 72-73
Exotic Revival-style, 84
French-style, 51
Gothic Revival, 60
Greek Revival, 23-26
Rococo Revival, 42-44, 47
Lincoln, Abraham, 27
Lincoln House, Vermont, 9